D0207527

UCONN STAMFORD LIBRARY
3 4012 01968 6075

THE CENTRAL AFRICAN REPUBLIC

PROFILES • NATIONS OF CONTEMPORARY AFRICA

Larry W. Bowman, Series Editor

The Central African Republic: The Continent's Hidden Heart, Thomas O'Toole

Lesotho: Dilemmas of Dependence in Southern Africa, John E. Bardill and James H. Cobbe

Botswana: Liberal Democracy and the Labor Reserve in Southern Africa, Jack Parson

Ethiopia: Transition and Development in the Horn of Africa, Mulatu Wubneh and Yohannis Abate

Kenya: The Quest for Prosperity, Norman N. Miller

Mozambique: From Colonialism to Revolution, 1900–1982, Allen Isaacman and Barbara Isaacman

Senegal: An African Nation Between Islam and the West, Sheldon Gellar

Tanzania: An African Experiment, Rodger Yeager

The Seychelles: Unquiet Islands, Marcus Franda

Swaziland: Tradition and Change in a Southern African Kingdom, Alan R. Booth

The Comoro Islands: Struggle Against Dependency in the Indian Ocean, Malyn Newitt

Ghana: Coping with Uncertainty, Deborah Pellow and Naomi Chazan

Somalia: Nation in Search of a State, David D. Laitin and Said S. Samatar

Cameroon, Mark W. DeLancey

The Ivory Coast, Barbara C. Lewis

Zambia, Marcia Burdette

Nigeria, Timothy M. Shaw

ABOUT THE BOOK AND AUTHOR

A small, poor, little-known nation, the Central African Republic has had a troubled history, from the days of slave raids by Arab-speaking peoples from the north, through the bizarre rule of Jean-Bedel Bokassa, to the present military regime. Landlocked and possessing few resources beyond its famed diamonds, it is one of the least developed nations in Africa. Since its independence from France in 1959, it has of necessity continued to depend on its former colonial ruler.

In this introduction to the Central African Republic, Dr. O'Toole examines the country's tumultuous past and current difficulties, the nature of the present political situation, and the roots of that situation in the colonial and precolonial periods. He also focuses on the roles of ethnicity, emerging urban problems, class formation, education, and religion in the social and cultural changes that the nation is currently undergoing. Finally, he realistically assesses the viability of the present government as a vehicle for economic development, stability, and reform.

Dr. O'Toole is a specialist on Francophone Africa. He has recently been a member of the faculty of Saint Cloud State University, Minnesota, where he was in the Department of Interdisciplinary Studies.

To Ann, Rachel, and Phillip,
whose support is total

THE CENTRAL AFRICAN REPUBLIC

The Continent's Hidden Heart

Thomas O'Toole

Westview Press • Boulder, Colorado

Gower • London, England

Profiles/Nations of Contemporary Africa

Published in 1986 in the United States of America by Westview Press, Inc.; Frederick A. Praeger, Publisher; 5500 Central Avenue, Boulder, Colorado 80301

Published in 1986 in Great Britain by Gower Publishing Company Limited, Gower House, Croft Road, Aldershot, Hampshire GU11 3HR

Library of Congress Cataloging-in-Publication Data
O'Toole, Thomas, 1941–
The Central African Republic.
(Profiles. Nations of contemporary Africa)
Bibliography: p.
Includes index.
1. Central African Republic. I. Title. II. Series.
DT546.322.086 1986 967 86-4099
ISBN (U.S.) 0-86531-564-7
ISBN (U.K.) 0-566-007738

Printed and bound in the United States of America

The paper used in this publication meets the minimum requirements of the American National Standard for Permanence of Paper for Printed Library Materials Z39.48-1984.

10 9 8 7 6 5 4 3 2 1

Contents

Tables, Maps, and Photographs

Tables

Maps

Photographs

Acknowledgments

A number of people served as my guides and mentors, facilitating my access to Central African society. The kindness of these people during and after my Fulbright year at the University of Bangui helped me, my wife, Ann, and our children, Rachel and Phillip, to see the Central African Republic "through other eyes."

I would like to thank the many Central Africans whose help and friendship made this book possible. I would especially like to thank Raphael Nzabakomada-Yakoma, François Sehoulia, Bernard Kouzoumna, Dieudonné Debry, Adolphe Pakoua, Joseph Ndakouzou, Jacqueline and Jean-Claude Salvador, Jonathan Ngaté, and Suzanne Goma-Ballou. I owe a tremendous intellectual debt to scholars who have studied the Central African Republic and have shared their ideas and research with me: Pierre Soumille, Dennis Cordell, Rita Headrick, Philip Noss, Thomas Christensen, and W. J. Samarin. Special thanks go to Pierre Kalck, whose guidance, support, and fully shared knowledge of Central Africa have been of inestimable assistance. I would also like to thank my teachers and fellow Africanists, Victoria Bomba Coifman, Allen Isaacman, and Lansiné Kaba, whose help and support in the beginning were invaluable.

Earlier drafts of this manuscript were edited and scrutinized by my good friend, Janice Baker. Michael Blake, Joe Hindman, Judy Brown, Gail McGee, Dan Vernon, Tim Rees, Alain Monteil, Herman and Giselle Pringnitz, Marie-Reine Déliot, Karen Woodbury, Rev. and Mrs. Don Hocking, Polly Strong, and Mary Bizot helped in a variety of ways both during and after my stay in Bangui.

I wish also to thank my mother, Dorothy, and my father, Philip, whose help and support have never failed. Though I have received much assistance on this book, any errors of fact or interpretation are mine.

Thomas O'Toole
Minneapolis, Minnesota

THE CENTRAL AFRICAN REPUBLIC

CENTRAL AFRICAN REPUBLIC

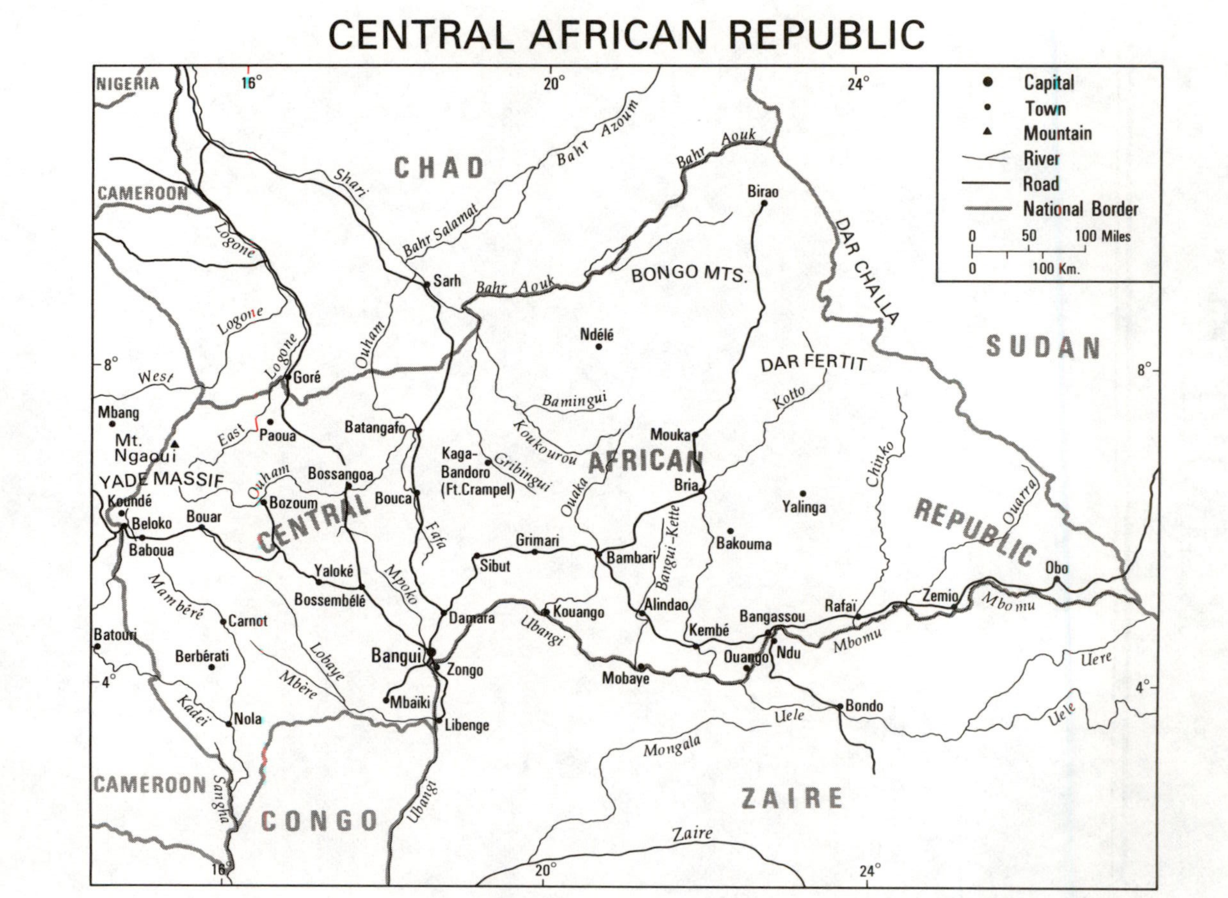

1

The Physical Setting

A LITTLE-KNOWN COUNTRY

No part of Africa, the world's second largest continent, has been more misunderstood, misrepresented, and mistreated over the years than the area that today constitutes the Central African Republic (CAR). All the stereotypes that once clouded European and North American perceptions of Africa have been applied with a vengeance to that portion of former French Equatorial Africa that bore the name Ubangi-Shari. Pygmies, jungles, heat, lions, and Ubangis with huge lip plugs—all these images and more make up the usual picture of Central Africa. These exotic images persist, even though the Aka (so-called Pygmies)[1] number around 16,000 and are virtually on the edge of extinction, the country's remaining tropical forest timber reserves are under severe pressure by foreign lumber companies, the heat is more tolerable than that in Washington, D.C., on a summer day, lions are rarely found outside the nation's game parks, and lip plugs are so few in number that most Central Africans have never seen one. The bizarre interlude of rule by Bokassa I, Africa's only twentieth-century emperor other than Ethiopia's Haile Selassie, dashed Central Africa's hopes to be more realistically understood.[2]

The Central African Republic's location in the very heart of the continent has profoundly affected its national development. The Republic lies almost exactly in the middle of the continent, just north of the equator. Bangui, the capital city, is about as far from Algiers, the capital of Algeria, as it is from Pretoria, the capital of the Republic of South Africa. The eastern half of the country is almost midway between the Atlantic Ocean and the

Red Sea. The majority of the country's population lives about the same distance from the Sahara Desert as they do from the equator. The CAR's location has made it a crossroads for more than two millennia of migration. Its geographic situation has also tended to restrict the development of a strong sense of national unity.

Today, the Central African Republic plays a minor role in world affairs. Its voting record at the United Nations shows little consistency. Its mineral resources—with diamonds the major exception—are scarcely surveyed, to say nothing of being tapped. Its soils produce far less than their limited potential. Its strategic importance to the French as a buffer against Libyan expansion ebbs and flows with the state of affairs in Chad. Finally, with a population of approximately 2,300,000, more than 40 percent of whom are under the age of fifteen, its human potential appears more a deficit than an asset.

Potentially, however, Central Africa's landlocked and isolated position could prove to be an asset. The 626,777-square-kilometer country shares accessible borders with five other countries. On the south a 3,500-kilometer border with the Congo and Zaire is partially defined by the Ubangi and Mbomu rivers. The Shari River partially defines the 2,300-kilometer northern border with Chad, but the 2,300-kilometer northeastern border with the Sudan and the shorter western border with Cameroon are scarcely defined by physical geography. Although most of the Central African Republic could be easily linked to population centers in neighboring countries by an improved road and railroad network, at present only one good road links it to Douala in Cameroon. When the rains are adequate, travel to the Atlantic Ocean is easier by boat down the Ubangi and Zaire rivers to Brazzaville and then by rail to Point-Noire, Congo.

Studies have been conducted for plans to extend the TransCameroonian Railway from Bélabo to Berbérati and even to create links to rail systems in Sudan and Gabon. The Central African States Development Bank decided in 1979 to support the TransCameroonian extension in principle. The United Nations Trans-African highway running from Lagos to Mombasa will pass through Bangui, and upgrading work has already begun with the help of an $18 million International Development Agency credit for road rehabilitation.

Bangui could become the hub of a truly viable common market area in the future, much as Switzerland was able to become a commercial and financial center for Europe. Bangui was the headquarters for the *Organisation Commune Africaine et Malgache—Organisation Commune Africaine et Mauricienne* (OCAM), which until 1972 sought to link the Francophone states of Africa into a common market. A number of specialized agencies spawned during OCAM's most active period continue to exist, and Bangui remains the seat of the *Union Douanière et Economique de l'Afrique Centrale* (UDEAC). UDEAC is a customs union that seeks to harmonize planning, industrial development, telecommunications, fiscal, and social policies among Gabon, Congo, Cameroon, and the Central African Republic. In October 1983, the Central African Republic joined Burundi, Cameroon, Chad, the Republic of Congo, Equatorial Guinea, Gabon, Rwanda, São Tomé and Príncipe, and Zaire in signing a treaty establishing the Economic Community of Central African States (ECOCAS) to promote economic and industrial cooperation. Central African leadership hopes that the union will stimulate industrial activity, increase markets, and reduce the country's dependence on France for trade and capital. Given the record of such cooperative efforts to date, immediate benefits for the majority of Central Africans from the ECOCAS would seem unlikely.

RELIEF

By and large the physical appearance of the county is not spectacular. Stretching from east to west across the center of the country is a high raised plateau that in the east separates the headwaters of two of the world's greatest rivers, the Zaire (Congo) and the Nile. In the northwest the Logone and Shari and their headwaters drain into the second largest interior drainage depression in the world, the Chad Basin. Most of this central plateau is a vast peneplain laced with river valleys and ranging in altitude from 600 to 700 meters. This gently rolling plain is covered with tropical savanna vegetation common to much of continental Africa outside the rain forest and the drier areas. Only isolated rock outcroppings (*kaga* in Sango, the national lingua franca), especially in the west, and occasional quartzite hogbacks and other harder rock structures break the expanse of the savanna plateau.

On the northern part of the frontier with Cameroon and along the entire frontier with Sudan there are mountainous areas. The Dar Fertit, Dar Challa, or Bongo Mountains in the northeast are elevated metamorphic rocks with rare isolated peaks. Here some elevations exceed 1,300 meters. Traveling from Bangui to the northwestern frontier with Cameroon and Chad, one crosses a series of gradually higher ridges composed chiefly of granite. The highest peak, Mount Ngaoui, on the Cameroon border, reaches 1,420 meters. To the southeast and also in the center of the eastern (Mouka-Ouadda) half of the country are two sandstone deposits that contain diamonds. In the Carnot Plateau in the southeast the sandstone ridges between relatively deep river valleys retain so little rainwater that they permit a Sudano-Guinean flora to penetrate into what would otherwise be tropical rain forest.

Given the abundance of fresh water in almost all seasons and some relatively good soils for a tropical area,[3] Central Africa has considerable agricultural potential. Along the northern border is a prolongation of the Chad depression, a comparatively fertile zone of sandy alluvial tracts. Considerable areas of alluvial soils are found along the upper reaches of the Ubangi River from the Lobaye to the Kotto rivers, along the Kadeï and Mbère rivers north of Nola to the Congo border, and along the Sangha River in the southwest as well.

WATERWAYS

The Central African Republic is drained by three great waterways. The northern third of the country forms part of the Chad Basin and is drained by tributaries of the Shari River. Ten percent of the country in the southwest is drained by the Sangha and its tributaries. The rest of the country, more than half its area, is drained by the Ubangi, the "great river." Flowing east to west from south of Bangassou in the southeastern part of the country for more than 500 kilometers, the Ubangi turns abruptly to the south at Bangui, the capital city, and flows about 700 kilometers to join the Zaire (Congo) River. Its headwaters, the Mbomu and the Uele, rising respectively 752 and 1,152 kilometers further east,

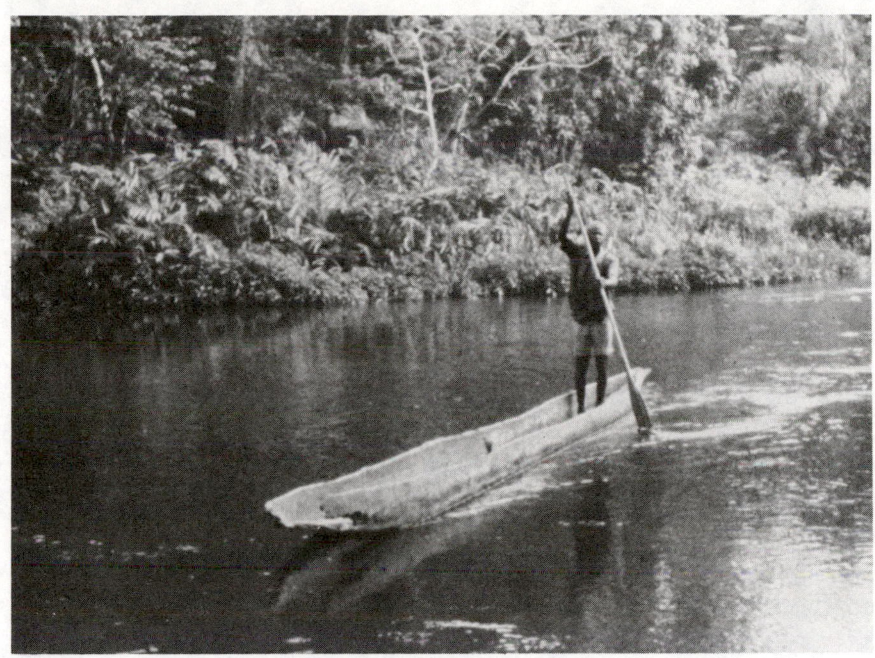

Aka in pirogue on the Ouham, a Shari River tributary. Photo courtesy of Barry Hewlett.

originate very close to the headwaters of the Nile. Draining this large well-watered area, the Ubangi has a tremendous volume of water. During the rainy season it flows at a rate of 10,000 cubic meters per second at Bangui.

The Sangha gets its name below Nola at the confluence of the Kadeï and Mbère. The valley of this river is more than 1,290 kilometers long. Along the ridge on either side of its valley are relatively dry savanna areas—one reason that the valley became a major communication link between the Zaire Basin, the original homeland of the Bantu, and later Muslim kingdoms.

The Shari River system dominates drainage to the Chad Basin, though the East and West Logone draining out of the Yadé Massif are themselves major rivers. The Shari's main tributaries are the Ouham, the Bamingui, and the Aouk. The Aouk, which rises in the Darfur, has a very uneven seasonal flow, while the Ouham, which rises in the Yadé Massif, has a greater abundance of fresh water in all seasons. The Gribingui, a major tributary of the Bamingui, was a major French access route to Chad in 1896.

CLIMATE AND VEGETATION

The climatic and vegetative zones of the Central African Republic virtually recapitulate those of the entire continent. All of Africa's climatic zones except the desert and Mediterranean belts are found stretched across Central Africa in horizontal bands. Bangui, the capital, is less than 500 kilometers from the equator, and Birao, the main town in the northeast, is the same distance from the desert. In the northeast the climate is the Sahelo-Sudanese type with a six-month dry season from November to April and with mean temperatures reaching 30°C in April and May. Here the rainfall averages 75 centimeters a year, and a remarkable variety of wild animals is found.

Between latitudes 7° and 5° north, an area that includes most of the Republic, the climate is far more humid. Here the number of dry months with less than 5 centimeters of rain between November and March varies from 5 in the north to 3 in the south. During the rains the savanna is green and, except in the Ubangi valley, the nights are often cool with frequent low-lying fog in the morning. At Bambari in the south central part of the country, the extreme temperatures recorded for December are 10° and 33°C. In general, annual rainfall increases from north to south, varying from less than 135 to 155 centimeters. Often these rains occur in very violent downpours of 8 to 10 centimeters in an hour.

South of latitutde 5° north the climate is equatorial. The dry season lasts three months or less, and in the thickly forested areas it rains year-round. At Berbérati (4° north), for example, the annual rainfall is approximately 165 centimeters. In general the humidity is high throughout the area, and the annual mean temperature is 25°C.

These three general climatic zones define three principal zones of vegetation. In the south, approaching the outskirts of Bangui and Berbérati, is the tropical rain forest. Though subject to heavy cutting in recent years, vast areas of this forest are still in their primeval condition. The northern fringe and other isolated areas within this zone are potentially rich agricultural areas for the production of hevea, cacao, kolanut trees, pepper plants, palm trees, coffee, and all kinds of subsistence crops. The middle savanna zone covers 242,000 square kilometers. Varying considerably from region to region, this grassland includes some of the best humid prairie for agriculture in Africa. Unfortunately much of the savanna has been ruined through overcropping of cotton and the destruction of vestigial dry forests in the southern valleys. The Sahelian climate of the north has hardly been tapped for agriculture, and the gum and shea butter produced there merit little consideration in the world market. Like much of the central savanna, this area was almost depopulated during the slave raids from 1860 to 1910.

POPULATION AND POLITICAL ETHNICITY

Contemporary research supports a de-emphasis of ethnographical preoccupations that caused most French administrators during the colonial period to attempt to separate Central Africans into fixed ethnic groups.[4] Overlapping groups, constant internal migrations, frequent miscegenation, orthographic errors, and poor research had led to much confusion. Central African ethnic groups, even more than in in many other parts of Africa are and have been historically open. Their membership and identity shift constantly. In the heterogeneous and diverse watershed area encompassed by the Central African Republic, ethnic groups have come together, changed, and disappeared continually throughout the past and still do so today.

Much of the Central African countryside today remains virtually unpopulated. The eastern third of the country has less than one person per three square kilometers. Many areas of the country remain simply large game parks devoid of any but transitory occupation. Throughout most of the more heavily populated parts of the country a similarity of customs and traditions, virtually identical patterns of social structure, and the wide diffusion of a single lingua franca, Sango, have in recent years tended to create an increasingly homogenous Central African culture. As towns have grown and better means of communication have been established, especially in the western half of the country, a relatively uniform culture has begun to develop out of the once diverse ethnicities of the various groups that have found refuge in the area over the past three to four centuries. Though some forest populations, certain highly Islamized groups, and a few cattle-keeping nomadic groups remain very unassimilated, most Central Africans today share a common basic culture. This is not to say that ethnic conflict does not play a role in the life of present-day Central Africans.

Most Central Africans live within an often disruptive but still persisting communitarian, lineage-based economic and political system. They can be mobilized to collective action by the country's small bureaucratic bourgeoisie for its ends by the "ethnicization" of deprivation or perceived threats. Ethnicization works in the following way: (1) The rise of the bureaucratic bourgeoisie at independence created a new social class. (2) This new social class wants to get the most out of their positions. (3) But this attempt is frustrated because French and other foreigners control most of the actual means of production and because there is a real scarcity of available resources so that the satisfaction of all members of the class is not possible. (4) This situation creates interclass conflicts within the bureaucratic bourgeoisie that are carried on in ethnic terms. Because the whole of the society is not fully stratified into rival social classes, individual members of the bureaucratic bourgeoisie activate or manipulate the latent ethnicity as the only available symbols for collective action.[5]

The Central Africans have suffered more than most other African peoples from the neglect, exploitation, and Europe-first orientation of the colonial policies. To date none of the governments of the Central African Republic has been able to overcome the consequences of a relatively sparse population. They have yet to find satisfactory ways to develop mineral, agricultural, and forest resources. To date the Central African Republic has not been able to obtain sufficient capital without giving up control of these resources to external agents. The past dreams of the continent-wide union that accompanied the independence movement in the late 1950s seem even more utopian today. Until the country finds ways to manage its own rich resources for the benefit of its people, the possibilities of economic and political stability for this small, landlocked nation seem remote.

NOTES

1. The widely used term "pygmy" is inherently pejorative and I prefer to use Aka, the name these people in the Central African Republic use for themselves. See Barry Hewlett et al., "Exploration Ranges of Aka Pygmies of the Central African Republic," *Man*, n.s. 17 (1983), 418–430.

2. See, for example, a basically pro-African Western journalist's view of Bokassa in David Lamb, *The Africans* (New York: Random House, 1982), 49–54.

3. Much of the geological and hydrological information in this chapter is drawn from Gérard Grellet, Monique Mainguet, and Pierre Soumille, *La République Centrafricaine* (Paris: Presses Universitaires de France, 1982), 7–52; and *Quarterly Economic Review of Gabon, Congo, Cameroon, Central African Republic, Chad, Equatorial Guinea* (London: The Economist Intelligence Unit Limited, 1984).

4. The treatment of ethnicity offered here and in Chapter 4 generally follows Dennis D. Cordell, "The Savanna Belt of North-Central Africa," in *History of Central Africa*, Vol. 1, ed. David Birmingham and Phyllis M. Martin (London: Longman, 1983), 30–74.

5. This understanding of the political aspects of "ethnicity" draws upon the closely parallel realities studied by Ilanga-Kabongo in "Ethnicity, Social Classes and the State in the Congo," (unpublished Ph.D. dissertation, Department of Political Science, University of California, Berkeley, 1973).

2

The Historical Context

FROM ORIGINS TO THE END OF THE SEVENTEENTH CENTURY

In the history of the Central African Republic there is a tremendous gap between events of the distant past, which can be traced in broad strokes using archaeological, geographical, and linguistic data, and events of the more recent past, which are documented by only a few written accounts and widely scattered traditions. Until very recently the area exhibited considerable cultural diversity. It appears that the historical processes that contributed to this diversity were complex. Furthermore, the data on them are scarce and the research studies few. Given the present state of knowledge, any generalizations about the earliest history of the area should be regarded as tentative. The working hypotheses advanced here are based on evidence currently available and are subject to radical revision as new data are found.[1]

As late as the 1930s it was commonly accepted that the area of the present-day Central African Republic had been a virtually uninhabited no-man's-land until nineteenth-century migrations filled the void. According to this view the only group that had any long-term residence in the area were people who called themselves the Aka. Known as Babinga by other Central African groups and Tvides by contemporary French scholars, these so-called pygmies were assumed to have occupied the equatorial forests in the country's southwestern extension long before the nineteenth century.

Culturally adapted to the forest and living a migratory existence, the Aka were perfect candidates for status as the country's aboriginal inhabitants. But in the early 1930s diamond- and gold-mining operations in the east and northeast of the country began to turn up obviously worked and polished flint and quartz tools found at different depths below the current earth's surface. It gradually became apparent that human occupation of the present-day CAR was of great antiquity. Based on careful studies conducted in the 1960s,[2] the conclusion now generally accepted is that fishing, hunting, and gathering populations have been present throughout most of the country for at least the past 8,000 years. The absence of human skeletal remains is apparently due to the high acidity of Central African soils rather than to any lack of long-term human occupation of the area.

Agricultural history suggests that the land in the Central African Republic was covered until the last millennium B.C. with a thick, dry forest that gave way to savanna only as agriculturalists slowly and laboriously cleared the land for millets and sorghums. By 2,500 years ago settled agricultural societies were established in the present-day Central African Republic. In the Bouar area several hundred groups of megaliths, large granite slabs standing upright and embedded in the soil near the banks of major streams, suggest that a sophisticated civilization existed in the area by that period. The size of the megaliths (in some cases several tons) and the complexity of their placement would have required enormous amounts of labor, indicating that they are the work of an advanced agricultural society.[3] Stone implements found far to the east in river valleys north of the Mbomu River confirm early settlements there, while investigations on the lower Logone and Shari rivers have also unearthed an important riverine civilization, termed the Sao, dating back more than a thousand years.

It would appear from linguistic studies that by A.D. 1400 the two major language groups presently found in the Central African Republic were already represented by a variety of peoples living in dispersed settlements. In the case of Central Sudanic language groups, it is likely these speakers had spread into southern Chad and northern and eastern Central African Republic well before 1400. Given the absence of natural obstacles between the Ubangi and the Nile valleys, there probably had been some linkage between these two areas since well before the present millennium. Even without entering the ongoing debate over the influence of Nile cultures on sub-Saharan Africa, it does appear likely that an intermittent trickle of immigrants from Kush and Meroe could well have contributed to the wide variety of peoples finding refuge between the Ubangi and Shari rivers.

Linguists currently maintain that a second language group, the Adamawa-Ubangian with a major branch on the Adamawa Massif, spread in a second branch called Ubangian eastward along the savanna north of the Ubangi River almost to the Great Lakes of East Africa. This dispersal probably dates back more than 1,000 years and could account for the band of long-inhabited settlement sites in the eastern part of the country, stretching along the Mbomu just north of the dense forest. Linguistic evidence indicates that these sites were occupied by relatively sedentary agriculturalists who already had iron-working skills upon arrival in the area or who developed this skill very soon after arrival. Practicing agricultural techniques mainly of West African origin, these Ubangian speakers occupied the wetter savannas along the fringes of the tropical forest to the south even before the Central Sudanic groups moved into the area. The narrow, well-populated strip in the Sangha and Lobaye valleys in the western part of the country, which links the northern grasslands with the southern Ubangi and Zaire basins and the Kinshasa grasslands, was also a major settlement area of these peoples in the first millennium A.D.

Written historical knowledge about today's Central African Republic begins to emerge from only the sixteenth century. There is still considerable controversy concerning the exact location and structure of a shadowy kingdom called Gaoga mentioned by the sixteenth-century traveler Leo Africanus. It is not known whether this problematic state—which Africanus claims had Christian populations, mounted horsemen, vast cattle herds, and numerous slaves—represented an actual, centralized monarchy including the eastern part of the present Central African Republic, or simply clusters of small states, or ephemeral kinship-based political congeries of pastoral peoples.

Much of the same incompleteness of information exists for a number of other semilegendary kingdoms that a variety of written sources posit to have existed in parts of the present Central African Republic. Anzica and a refugee outpost of Aloa, the last Christian kingdom of Nubia, remain today almost as little known or understood as they were in the sixteenth century when, as the mythical kingdom of Prester John, they lured the Portuguese to penetrate Africa from both the west and the east.[4] In any case, the social organization of most savanna societies until at least 1400 inhibited the growth of centralized authority. Whatever centralization did exist was rare and was probably a response to specific outside stimuli among basically very decentralized populations. This is not to say that societies in the northern savanna were not influenced by trans-Saharan contacts before 1400, but with the exception of some slave raiding into the northern fringes of the CAR, little direct contact existed before the seventeenth century.

By the year 1600 three fairly stable Islamicized states had emerged or reemerged to the north and partially extended into present-day Central African Republic. Darfur, Wadai, and Bagirmi all interacted with North Africa and responded like the Hausa states farther west to the waxing and waning of more powerful states that bounded them on the east (Nile) and the west (Kanem-Bornu). The impact of these states and the expansion of the trans-Saharan system on the Central African Republic as these states raided south for slaves before 1700 remains largely unknown. In most areas violence and flight were the major responses of the peoples of today's Central African Republic. Furthermore, the introduction of diseases such as smallpox, syphilis, and measles among the nonimmune populations must have caused significant depopulation in some areas.[5]

THE EIGHTEENTH AND NINETEENTH CENTURIES

Geographically situated on the periphery of the trans-Saharan trade and on the ancient Nile and Red Sea routes to India, the present-day Central African Republic was among the last areas of sub-Saharan Africa to be fully drawn into the world economy. The global economy that had begun to take shape in the fifteenth century as the new capitalist commercial system of Northwest Europe began expanding around the world did not directly penetrate Central Africa until the late eighteenth and early nineteenth centuries. Yet even before the European military domination of Central Africa had been accomplished in the twentieth century, externally oriented commercial networks, especially those directed toward the Atlantic coast, had created complex relationships among differing African interests propelling the world economy into the heart of Central Africa.

The history of the peoples of Central Africa for the past five hundred years has been dominated by competition. Peoples with common languages and customs have vied with one another for advancement and sometimes even for survival throughout the period. The urgency of this competition might reflect a background of fundamental scarcity originally created by drought, disease, and the inability of a basically hunting and gathering economy complemented by yam culture to assure a plentiful food supply. Even in the areas where millets and sorghums replaced the yams, harvests often withered in drought and fell prey to pests. The myth of a "tropical treasure trove" was never realized among the marginal Central African agriculturalists. Rainfall, human fertility, and the lack of animal-drawn plows were key issues even before external forces increased the pressure on relatively scarce resources. Living close to the soil and relying on rain and rudimentary tools, the Central African people were always vulnerable to changing ecological conditions. Scarcity, though neither constant nor present in all places, often provoked conflict.

Faced with the dramatic expansion of external trade from the fifteenth through the nineteenth centuries, Central Africans gradually found themselves caught up in rivalries that wracked the various peoples that were involved in the trade. Some fought against expansion, and some fled. Many others, however, welcomed the change. People of every category turned the new opportunities to old ends. They adopted imported weapons and defended their own ways of gaining wealth and power. Fear of defeat by local and neighboring rivals drove Africans to seek advantage for themselves, their kin, and their allies through contacts with the overseas markets for African labor and produce. The unexpected cost of such commitments created new conflicts and further increased the pressure on the scarce food-resource base of the local societies. For most people in the area Central Africa's increasing participation in the world economy had a largely negative effect. Some indigenous groups and persons, however, did profit, using connections with the exterior to further interests of their own groups.

The major wealth that Central Africa had to offer the world economy was its human population. Though some Central Africans had probably been taken north as slaves along the Nile trade routes before the Christian era and certainly many were transported in the trans-Saharan trade before 1700, it was not until the late eighteenth century that the export of human beings from Central Africa became an important element in world trade. Beginning in the mid-seventeenth century, the trans-Saharan slave trade, which had for centuries been a trickle, became a human flood pouring across the desert. At the same time an increasing flow of this living cargo began to be transported by rivers to the southeast, where they became part of the Atlantic slave trade. By the nineteenth century enslaved people from the area were also being traded to the east coast of Africa as part of the Indian Ocean trade.

The pull of the Atlantic slave trade, like the trans-Saharan trade, had probably begun to influence the area of the present Central African Republic well before the eighteenth century. It was only during the late eighteenth century, however, that an indigenous trading diaspora seized the opportunities for profit offered by this trade and developed widespread and intensive commercial networks with what had been largely autonomous groups and villages. By 1880 the Bobangi (for whom the Ubangi River is named), a loose conglomerate of riverine peoples, had formed a strong commercial network of which the major function was supplying slaves and some ivory through Tio intermediaries to the Atlantic coast for shipment to the Americas. Oral traditions dating to at least the latter half of the nineteenth century tell of large canoes with a capacity of fifty or more people that plied the southwestern rivers of the country, trading imported goods such as cloth, beads, guns, powder, and jewelry for people when possible, and raiding villages and capturing the inhabitants or stealing children and other unwary individuals when necessary. The people who were freely traded were often troublemakers or people who for some reason were poorly assimilated into the local population. Yet tremendous dislocations occurred as the trade intensified. The generally predatory nature of the exchange between the river people and the Gbaya, Manja, and other peoples of the interior became more and more acute as prices paid for slaves increased and supplies diminished.[6] Fear of capture prompted people to abandon their fields and villages and led, by the end of the nineteenth century, to a partial breakdown of societal organization throughout much of the Sangha and Lobaye watersheds. The animosity between the river peoples and the groups among whom they raided continues even today. Present political difficulties are influenced by the fact that the riverine groups, having the earliest direct access to European education, make up the bulk of the elite bureaucratic bourgeoisie that has dominated Central African politics for the past four decades.

Further east, however, beyond direct contact with the Atlantic system, results of the growth in trade were different. The introduction of New World food crops here had a major demographic effect on African societies. Maize and manioc (cassava) began to replace indigenous millets and sorghums sometime after 1700. Increased agricultural productivity among peoples of the Mbomu and Chinko river valleys allowed an Azande elite group, the Avongara, to establish a series of large chiefdoms in the eastern part of present-day Central African Republic. Likewise the Bandia, a Ngbandi clan, came to rule over Azande, Nzakara, and a mixed collection of other peoples from the late seventeenth through the nineteenth centuries in an area just west of the major Azande cultural zone.

With the decline of the Atlantic slave trade after the outlawing of the commerce in Brazil in the 1850s, the level of violence abated in the southwestern regions. But an intensification of the slave trade in the northern savanna—among the Gbaya, Manza, Sara, and Banda—led to increased conflict elsewhere after 1850. For the most part Muslim merchants connected with the Saharan caravan trade directed this northern commerce. The northern savanna had been linked tenuously with desert trade from an early date through the well-developed states between Lake Chad and the Nile—Kanem-Bornu in the lake area, Bagirmi to the east in what is today central Chad, and Wadai and Darfur located respectively to the east and west of the current Chad-Sudan border. Beginning in the eighteenth century, these states sent raiders south into Mbum, Sara, and Banda lands to seize slaves and ivory.[7]

Each of these states had its informal raiding preserve: Kanem-Bornu raided among the Mbum-Karre-Panha in the west, and the Bagirmi warriors went south to capture Sara slaves. Wadaians plundered the Nduka, Kara, Gula, and Banda south of their territory, while the Fursians wreaked havoc among the peoples of the northeastern Ubangi-Shari and the southwestern Nile basins.

During the period of slave raids small numbers of Muslim merchants trading in "legitimate" goods such as cloth, tea, sugar, perfume, and salt began to appear in the area. Small commercial centers that later gave way to or were replaced by colonial bases grew up in the early nineteenth century at places like Kale just west of Ndélé and at Mbele further west. The foundation of a strong, potentially viable, indigenous commercial sector was well underway before the colonial presence began to manifest itself.

Although the violence of the raiding associated with the desert trade should be neither overlooked nor underestimated, it is important to note that raids were not continuous. The northerners came south only several times annually, nearly always in the dry season when the rivers were low and the routes free from high savanna grass. Although the commerce brought violence, it also introduced the peoples of these regions to products from the outer world, to news of other places, and to a world religion, Islam. For better or worse, by 1880 the northern part of the Ubangi-Shari had been integrated into the desert system and through it into the European and Muslim worlds at large.

Although it is difficult to quantify the trade, small caravans of ivory hunters and traders from the area of modern Tanzania and Kenya probably were penetrating the headwaters of the Mbomu River and farther north by the mid-nineteenth century. Warfare and slave raiding moved with these traders because the caravans raided and traded to get porters for their ivory as a matter of course. The same skills needed for elephant hunting proved valuable in the capture of humans. Before much-improved firearms became available in the 1870s and 1880s these spear-wielding elephant killers had to be highly skilled and physically fit. Yet this intrusion of frontiersmen from the Indian Ocean trade network, though very disruptive further east, was overshadowed in the Ubangi region by the far heavier onslaught of alien traders from Egypt and North Africa.

In the nineteenth century Muslim slave raiding and trading and commerce in ivory and firearms coming from the north were the major influences on the history of the region. Fear of raiders caused the migration of many groups of people into Ubangi-Shari and also prompted internal movement. The Gbaya-Manja, who may originally have lived in the Adamawa savanna of central Cameroon, began moving east in the early part of the century to escape Fulbé (Bororo) raids. Oral traditions among various Banda groups indicate that they came from the western Sudan and today's Sudan–Central African frontier area. Although they never acted in a unified fashion, the many Banda groups began arriving in Ubangi-Shari early in the nineteenth century to escape marauders from Darfur. Yet none of these peoples escaped the raiders definitively. In the latter part of the century the demand for African slaves in the Muslim world increased, in part as a consequence of the Russian colonization of the Caucasus, which eliminated a traditional source of captives for Middle Eastern markets.

In response to this renewed and enlarged demand, one of the traditional Nile valley traders or *jallaba,* al-Zubayr Rahma Mansur, organized groups of previously disparate caravan guards into a private standing army and established his headquarters well south of the Bahral-Ghazal. He soon so dominated the trade that he was recognized by Egypt as governor of Bahral-Ghazal, thus creating a secondary empire within a secondary empire. Only when he conquered Darfur in 1874 and established his trans-Saharan commercial outlet did Egypt step in, and finally in 1878 the Khartoum government absorbed this trading empire.

One unit of Zubayr's forces under the command of Rabih Fadlallah moved west in 1879. At first his army, made up of captured and purchased recruits but armed with breech-loading rifles, pushed south toward the Mbomu valley where they came into conflict with Bari, the father of Bangassou, the famous sultan of the Nzakara in the early colonial period. Following the fall of Zubayr, Rabih settled in northeastern Ubangi-Shari on the Yata River and occupied the high rock plateau at Ouanda-Djale, an excellent defensive position that commanded important trade routes. He brought local Kara warriors into his ranks, raided for slaves among the Gula further west, and traded them to Muslim merchants for firearms. His power grew and in 1880 he headed west to the area of Dar al-Kuti, a client state of the northern Wadai Empire.

Rabih spent about a decade in Ubangi-Shari and the Chad Basin, raiding among the Banda and Sara peoples and training his forces. Suspicious of Rabih's intentions in his southern domains, the Wadai sultan disrupted trade on the routes connecting the area with the desert caravan network. This blockade prompted Rabih to attack Sultan Bari on the Mbomu River in 1883, hoping to open a southern route to the Muslim Zanzibari traders in the northeastern Congo Basin, with whom he could exchange slaves for firearms and munitions.

Rabih's peregrinations continued in the region until the early 1890s. In 1890 he removed Kobur, the Wadai client, from the throne of Dar al-Kuti, and installed Kobur's nephew, Muhammad as-Sanusi, as sultan. He cemented the alliance with the new ruler by giving him a wife and taking a daughter of the sultan to be his son's wife. He then moved west and captured Bagirmi in 1893 and defeated the Wadai army sent to capture him. With the capture of Bornu in 1894 Rabih moved his field of operations out of the confines of the modern-day Central African Republic. He was ultimately defeated in 1900 by three columns of soldiers under French command from Algeria, French Sudan, and Ubangi.

As-Sanusi, whom Rabih had left behind to rule Dar al-Kuti from his capital at Ndélé, proved to be even more rapacious. The raiding zone of this state, which grew to be the largest precolonial state in the area, reached from the present-day Sudan–Central African frontier to the Ubangi River.

The sultanate grew from a small cluster of settlements along the Jangara River northwest of Ndélé until it incorporated the trading sultans along the Mbomu and the Salamat region of southeastern Chad. It expanded in the manner of other precolonial states in the area: Raiding served to increase the population concentrated at Ndélé because as-Sanusi resettled many of his captives there, incorporating young men and boys into his armies and giving women as wives and concubines to his officers. He gave other captives to foreign Muslim traders in exchange for rare and costly trade goods. By judicious gift giving he used these goods to assure the loyalty of his followers. So profitable was the operation and so numerous the captives for sale that small groups of traders from the Nile region, Wadai, Kanem-Bornu, Hausaland, and even Libya had established themselves in Ndélé by 1900.

Although the history of northwestern Ubangi-Shari in the nineteenth century is also a tale of raiding, it ended differently. The Fulbé raids that provoked the Gbaya migrations continued well into this century. Adama, a Fulbé political leader, carrying on the jihad tradition launched by Usuman dan Fodio, set up his capital at Yola on the Benue River in present-day Nigeria, and in 1835 one of his lieutenants, Zody, settled at Ngaoundéré, an ancient Mbum center. Adama levied an annual tax on Ngaoundéré to be paid in slaves. Zody obtained these captives by raiding the Mbum and the Gbaya. These campaigns continued for a half century, and Ngaoundéré became for the Gbaya and Mbum regions what Zubayr's center had been for the eastern peoples, and Ndélé for the northern Banda—a base of military and commercial operations, and an assembly point for slaves.

In 1880 the Gbaya and Mbum finally began to organize themselves to resist the Fulbé. Several local leaders who had lived among the Fulbé and knew their customs and military tactics led the resistance. Internal quarrels among the Fulbé had also weakened their power, and by 1890 they could barely control the trade route joining Ngaoundéré with Kounde and Ouesso further south.

Although the slave trade developed as a response to an external demand for captives and led to the operations of foreign Muslims like al-Zubayr, Rabih, and Zody, the traffic depended upon the co-option and cooperation of indigenous chiefs and warriors. Rabih's forces were in large measure composed of Kara and Kresh, two other peoples of the western Ubangi-Shari who were exterminated in the fighting during the last century. As-Sanusi's bands included many Banda warriors, and Gbaya raiders also joined the Fulbé raiders in the northwest.

This late nineteenth century commerce in slaves had two destructive effects: It set indigenous peoples against each other, and it contributed to the depopulation of the area. Both effects have left their mark on the Central African Republic today. Undoubtedly the traffic in slaves is partially responsible for the animosity between Muslims and non-Muslims in the north and northwest. As for depopulation, a glance at the map quickly indicates the problem. The central and eastern regions of the country have few settlements and roads partly because the population is not dense enough to permit the development of infrastructure such as transportation, commerce, health services, education, and administration. Though this demographic imbalance is, to some extent, the result of environmental change and the potential offered by food crops of the Americas, other major reasons for the drastic population decline in the area are war casualties, slave raiding, and out-migration in the late nineteenth century caused by intensified Muslim raiding for the human wealth of the area.

THE COMING OF THE EUROPEANS AND THE COLONIAL ERA, 1899–1940

In the last two decades of the nineteenth century the shift from slave trade to an economic system based on the selling of manufactured goods and the extraction of raw materials began to change the attitudes of the major European powers toward Africa. Coal-burning ships shortened the travel time and increased cargo capacity. The use of quinine to control malaria allowed Europeans to survive in the tropics. Breech-loading and finally automatic rifles and rudimentary machine guns gave them the "tools of expansion." Increasing competition for markets and raw materials led France, Germany, Belgium, and Britain to seek military and political control over African territories. The present-day Central African Republic did not figure high on the list of areas to be controlled by the two colonial superpowers, France and Britain. Only because equatorial Africa was a back door to Lake Chad and the Nile did the French government show any interest in the area. Failing to create a band of French territory from the Atlantic to the Indian Ocean and wrest control of the Upper Nile from the British after the confrontation at Fashoda in 1898, the French turned their attention once more to the Chad basin. They ultimately claimed the Central African savanna as an adjunct to an imperial desire first voiced by Savorgnan de Brazza in the 1880s to create a vast empire uniting French West Africa, Algeria, and the area north of the Congo (Zaire) River. French expeditionary forces occupied Ubangi-Shari in 1889, but British and German claims limited attempts to control the far more fertile and densely populated Cameroon highlands.

At the Conference of Berlin (1884-1885) King Leopold II of Belgium had attempted to claim all of the Ubangi drainage area by presenting doctored maps that deliberately left out this major river as a potential frontier. Based on the early explorations of Savorgnan de Brazza in the Sangha valley in the early 1880s, Albert Dolisie's trip up the Zaire to the Ubangi confluence in 1886, and other information, a Franco-Leopoldian convention recognized French rights to the north bank of the Ubangi. The French founded Bangui as part of the French Congo colony in 1899 to counterbalance the post the Belgians had established across the river at Zongo as an outpost of the Congo Free State. The Mbomu, Uele, Chinko, and Kouango basins continued to be disputed areas until another accord between France and Leopold II fixed the Mbomu rather than the Uele as the frontier between their possessions. In these, as in other colonial territorial disputes, the African people of the area played little or no part in the negotiations.

In 1905 administrative responsibility for Ubangi-Shari (which was to become, at independence, the Central African Republic) along with that for Chad, Gabon, and Moyen-Congo was placed under a governor-general stationed at Brazzaville. In 1910 Ubangi-Shari joined the two French colonies, Gabon and Moyen-Congo and Chad (the colonial status of which was not fixed until 1920) to form the federation of French Equatorial Africa (*Afrique Equatoriale Française,* AEF). The governor-general was named by the French government and was given broad administrative powers over the federation, including control of local civil, military, and judicial services and all communications with the French minister of the colonies. The governor-general, in addition to his responsibility for internal and external defense, also controlled economic and financial matters with AEF. Like the other colonies, Ubangi-Shari had a lieutenant governor. The governor-general was assisted by an administrative council and an aide who, with the title of colonial governor, served as secretary-general for AEF. Between 1910 and the outbreak of World War II, a succession of seven governors-general served in the administration of AEF.

The administrative structure in Ubangi-Shari duplicated that of the government in Brazzaville, including the secretary-general and an appointed advisory council. The lieutenant governor was empowered to construct the Ubangi-Shari budget under tight control of the central administration in Brazzaville. By the 1930s the lieutenant governor of Ubangi-Shari was simply an administrative delegate following orders from Brazzaville. Nominal decentralization was unsuccessfully attempted six times between 1910 and 1946. Although military administrators were replaced by civilians and changes were made in boundary lines, names, and sizes of administrative units, Brazzaville's control over Ubangi-Shari remained; predominantly meaningful reforms affecting decentralization did not come until after World War II.

The areas drained by the Sangha and the Ouham in the western part of the Ubangi-Shari also entered the colonial era as an arena for the more widespread competition between Germany and France for territorial possessions. Bangui was cut off from the Moyen-Congo from 1911 until 1914 by Neu-Kamerun, a salient to the Zaire River through western Central African Republic, which was granted to Germany as part of the settlement surrounding the Moroccan crisis of 1911. When Cameroon was divided between France and Britain after World War I, the area of Neu-Kamerun again reverted to France according to Article 119 of the Versailles Treaty (June 28, 1919), although the Haute-Sangha and Lobaye areas were not definitively incorporated under Bangui administration until the 1930s.

Agreements between colonial powers and the creation of a plan for administering Ubangi-Shari were not automatically ratified by the African people living within the arbitrarily defined boundaries of the colony. The French "pacification" of Ubangi-Shari took a series of military campaigns that occurred sporadically during the first three decades of the twentieth century. No established trade or mineral interests existed in the Ubangi-Shari region. Consequently, most local government was abandoned to the private interests of concessionary companies. Acknowledging the impotence of colonial government in the area, the French government in 1899 leased more than half of the territory of Ubangi-Shari to seventeen newly created concessionary companies that were then given virtually free rein to exploit the labor and natural products of the area. A poorly trained and underfinanced colonial administration created a highly authoritarian, largely ineffectual, and often brutal regime. Whether as part of German dreams of a great *Mittelafrika* linking Kamerun with German East Africa, or as part of early French dreams for an Atlantic-to-Red Sea empire, or a later French plan for a Congo-to-Mediterranean linkage, or as simply the periphery of Leopold's Congo Free State, most of the present-day Central African Republic suffered a merciless concessionary exploitation during the first decades of European occupation. Though already demoralized and shattered by generations of Muslim invasions, not all Central Africans accepted this European occupation of their land. From mid-1906 until September 1909, for example, a Vridri leader, Baram-Bakié, conducted a successful armed resistance to the French colonial forces in the area south of Bambari. Using modern arms and well-established fortified villages, this courageous Central African leader consciously sought to maintain his authority over a number of villages between Bambari and the Ubangi River.[8] This and numerous other smaller acts of armed resistance to colonial occupation between 1900 and 1920 give lie to the myth of French "pacification" being a boon for the people of Central Africa.

From the beginning, in order to turn a profit the agents of the concessionary companies used whatever constraints they deemed necessary to force local populations to collect wild rubber and ivory. The few French administrators present in this colonial backwater seldom attempted to enforce laws against forced labor because their own attempts to squeeze out enough taxation through head taxes and customs duties to support the regime often went hand in hand with the labor exactions of the concessionaries. Maintaining the myth that left to their own devices Africans would work only enough to survive, colonial administrators rationalized that the head tax and its concomittant forced labor were necessary components of the economic development of the colonies. Under the initial massive onslaught of profiteering, wild rubber vines soon became scarce. As world markets for rubber declined in the first decade of the twentieth century, many companies went bankrupt. Profits continued only where the most brutal agents continued to direct their African auxiliaries to increase violence, torture, and hostage holding in order to force local people to collect the increasingly rare rubber at ever-higher human costs.

By 1920 most of the people in the western third of the modern Central African Republic suffered from famine, social disruption, and a variety of indigenous and introduced diseases. In spite of a brief attempt to ameliorate conditions, launched in France during the 1920s, the continued pressures to make the colony self-supporting and also yield profits for the private concessionary companies caused conditions to worsen for the mass of the population. The labor demands for the Congo-Ocean Railroad in 1925 and 1926 caused further disruption as tens of thousands of men in the prime of life were taken by force to work a thousand kilometers from their homes. Between 1928 and 1931 a series of largely localized and disconnected incidents of armed resistance flared up in the Haute-Sangha and Lobaye districts and surrounding areas. Attacking European and other intrusive commercial and administrative personnel, various local groups sought immediate relief from the labor and economic exactions forced on them by the profit seekers who formed the backbone of colonial occupation. Urged on by local colonialists, the colonial administration of AEF and the Cameroon protectorate crushed all real and supposed anticolonial activity. Maintaining that they were faced with an organized, massive outbreak of violence, the colonial administration justified the use of overwhelming force to do away with any possibility of further armed resistance to either government or concessionary exploitation in Ubangi-Shari. Bent on definitely "pacifying" the area, the French administration and colonists in the area created the specter of a centrally directed, widespread threat to law and order to avoid the bad publicity that a careful examination of the oppression and exploitation inherent in the concessionary system would have caused.[9]

By the mid-1930s the economic stagnation of the AEF in general and especially Ubangi-Shari was an embarrassment to the French government. Modeled upon policies in the Belgian Congo, an attempt was launched by the French government to promote the growing of cotton in Ubangi-Shari. This was done in order to create an autonomous source of a vital industrial raw material that would otherwise have to be imported from non-French areas. Though it placed a great strain upon the fragile savanna ecology and was opposed by both the surviving concessionaires and knowledgeable colonial administrators for fear of its negative impact upon African food production, increased amounts of cotton were produced through coercion. This is a tyical example of many such enterprises that fitted the logic of imperial strategy but made little sense in economic terms and caused a great deal of suffering for the population of Ubangi-Shari. Coffee production also showed some promise until a blight (tracheomycosis) destroyed most of the newly created plantations in 1938; production of gold and diamonds increased sporadically during this period. In almost every instance, however, production, or at least the commercialization of production, was in the hands of Europeans. The colonial administration remained far more interested in extracting taxes than in helping local populations to profit from increased production.

One major source of pride for the French during the colonial period was their health services. Accepting responsibility for the spread of sleeping sickness as a result of the greater movement of people following French penetration and fearing a loss of even more scarce laborers, the French administration advanced considerable sums to fight the disease from the late 1920s. Mobile health units created to fight sleeping sickness brought better medical care to rural populations than would otherwise have been the case. It was not until the mid-1930s and especially after World War II, however, that comprehensive maternal and child-care clinics and multipurpose health services replaced the single-minded emphasis on sleeping sickness. But the groundwork of African male nurses and rural health care had been established.[10]

Other social services, especially education, were mostly left to Christian missionaries. The French administration in Ubangi-Shari feared creating a class of potentially unruly, educated, unemployed Africans. Consequently, state education was extremely limited through the mid-1930s and missionary efforts at education were often harassed by administration officials and regulations. Because of limited funds and an apparent prejudice against equatorial Africans, the backward nature of education in Ubangi-Shari persisted through independence.

WORLD WAR II AND ITS AFTERMATH

France's declaration of war on the Third Reich on September 1, 1939, had little immediate effect on Ubangi-Shari. Prime Minister

Henri Pétain's surrender to the Germans on June 17, 1940, and Brigadier General Charles de Gaulle's subsequent call to fight on were far more momentous events. Procrastinating until August 30, 1940, the French governor of Ubangi-Shari, Governor Auguste Saint-Mart, finally placed the colony of Ubangi-Shari in the Free French camp after the neighboring colonies of Cameroon, Chad, and Congo had already declared for de Gaulle. Saint-Mart's vacillation was a normal reaction to the unclear state of affairs in the summer of 1940. On July 21 a group of French recruits had seized the ammunition depot at Bangui and had been arrested by officers loyal to Marshal Pétain. In fact, Commander Henri Cammas of the Bangui garrison held the camp for the Vichy government until September 3. Faced with the threat of armed attack by reservists and troops from Bouar who had gone over to the Free French, Commander Cammas surrendered. He and a few supporters were allowed to return to France by way of Portugal.

Ultimately, African troops recruited from the colonies served with distinction and valor in Syria and North Africa. At the battle of Bir Hacheim, Lieutenant Jean-Marie Koudoukou's valor earned him a posthumous *Croix de la Libération;* he was the first African to be so decorated. Ten percent of the 3,000 Africans who left Ubangi-Shari to fight for the French never returned.

Under Felix Eboué, General de Gaulle's appointee as governor-general of AEF, some political reforms were attempted in Ubangi-Shari during the war. Eboué was a black, Guyanese-born civil servant who had served in the Ubangian countryside from 1909 to 1921 and from 1923 to 1931 and had always desired to grant some measure of local control to Africans. His attempt to establish a system of indirect rule through traditional leaders was largely unsuccessful. The disruption caused by the slave trade, the Muslim invasions, and the impact of the concessionary regime had virtually eliminated the base of traditional authority.

Ubangi-Shari actually benefited from the war economically. In order to aid the war effort the French built better roads throughout the colony, and the river port and airport at Bangui were improved. Furthermore, British markets for locally produced goods, no longer controlled by French demands, added to a general prosperity for the colony. Diamond, cotton, and coffee production went up and the collection of wild rubber was again undertaken.

Of course, almost all of this expansion was at the expense of increased labor by the local population. In effect, the regime returned to a concessionary system. European cotton merchants were granted purchase monopolies over cotton produced by local populations under government coercion, and transportation and exportation monopolies became more firmly fixed in the hands of the European commercial societies that had evolved from the earlier concessionary companies.

Nevertheless, French Equatorial Africa emerged from World War II a very different place than it had been before the war. The widespread participation of Central Africans in Free French campaigns in North Africa, Southwest Asia, and Europe had an as yet incompletely studied effect upon this previously isolated colonial enclave. The stories, impressions, and opinions of these returned soldiers had a definite influence on large numbers of Central Africans. Returning to their families and villages, these *anciens combattants* were far more aware than any preceding generation that an administrative entity called Ubangi-Shari existed and that they, whatever their ethnic origin, were perceived by the world at large as "Ubangians" rather than Gbaya, Manja, or Banda. Sharing strong ties with their fellow comrades, they represented a new social group, almost a separate class, which presented a unified front on a number of social, economic, and political questions.[11]

TOWARD INDEPENDENCE WITH BOGANDA

The several thousand French colons who had firmly established themselves in Ubangi-Shari by 1946 immediately felt the political and economic changes the war had catalyzed. At the end of the war French was in ruins, and its recovery appeared to depend upon the development of the franc zone as a self-sufficient economic system. The AEF had rallied to the Free French, and at a 1944 conference in Brazzaville, de Gaulle had announced major reforms of France's relations with its overseas possessions aimed at creating more dynamic ties between the metropole and its tropical dependencies. Under the 1946 constitution of the new Fourth Republic, Africans were granted citizenship in their own overseas section of the French Union, though not on an equal footing with natives of France. At the same time the wartime boom had offered the opportunity for many more Africans to enter commerce, transportation, and timber-cutting and small scale commercial farming operations. Capital gained in service professions and military service allowed a few hundred Ubangians to begin to expand a medium-range enterprise sector that had previously been lacking. These activities became important in political terms, because they increased competition and friction between the European colons and Africans.

From an economic perspective neither Ubangians nor French settlers were building on very firm ground. By the early 1950s France had managed a very impressive economic recovery, but little of it was the result of AEF contributions. The declining terms of international trade and the high cost of transportation made tropical raw materials from Ubangi-Shari less than competitive. The illusion of prosperity created by a major series of postwar development projects instituted by the French government in Ubangi-Shari and elsewhere under the FIDES (*Fonds d'Investissement pour le Développement Economique et Social*) program gradually wore off by the mid-1950s. Few French settlers and almost no Africans had sufficient capital to bring about a qualitative transformation of the production base. The increased public capital for funded projects and some increased external investment in the mining sector created the illusion of growth in the Ubangi-Shari economy through the late 1940s and early 1950s. For a time relatively large amounts of labor and provisions were required and a deceptive boom was created. In the long run, as individual African cultivators produced no more efficiently, as world market demands expanded slowly if at all, and as no viable internal markets evolved, the public debt from metropolitan subsidies grew faster than increased productive capacity. Post–World War II transportation projects were more costly than older ones that had used forced labor and created far less impact on the economy than the first roads. Many of the development projects launched in the early years of FIDES, especially those in agriculture, proved not to be viable in the long run. It is against this background of growing need for new taxation and subventions from the metropole that the constitutional changes, party struggles, and emerging national leaders that marked the period between 1946 and independence in 1960 must be viewed.

Although it is true that the constitution of the Fourth Republic adapted on October 13, 1946, radically altered the rules for politics in Ubangi-Shari, it is also true that French settlers there and elsewhere in the French colonial world had used their considerable political leverage to assure that the document was far more conservative than the recommendations adopted by the conference convened by General de Gaulle at Brazzaville in January 1944. In the 1946 constitution the worst injustices such as the *indigenat* legal system (the harsh, racist rules of French police administration over African people as per decrees of May 31, 1910, and December 31, 1925) and the corvée (forced labor) were abolished. Africans lost their subordinate status as subjects, and Ubangi-Shari (as well as other colonies of AEF) became an overseas territory of France. Each territory was granted the right to elect a territorial assembly with limited powers, which in turn was to elect delegates to a French general council to be established for all of AEF. In addition, each territory was granted the right to elect representatives to the parliamentary bodies of the government of the French republic, including the National Assembly, the Council of the Republic, and the Assembly of the French Union. The position of governor-general of AEF was redesignated high commissioner.

All of these constitutional provisions, however, did little to change effectively the real flow of authority. Policy decisions continued to emanate from Paris. Only 100,000 Africans were allowed to vote in AEF; a separate electoral college was limited to individuals previously holding French citizenship, mainly local Europeans. No attempt was made to train Africans for civil service positions. The reliance on French personnel for administrative and technical positions continued through independence and, in many fields, right up to the present.

On November 10, 1946, the first Ubangian deputy, Barthélemy Boganda, was elected to the French National Assembly by 9,000 of the approximately 20,000 Africans (former French soldiers, "chiefs," and *evolués*—Western-educated Africans who had adopted a French life-style) allowed to vote in Ubangi-Shari.[12] From 1946 until his death in 1959 Boganda played a major role in the politics of Ubangi-Shari and justifiably bears the title of "father" of his country. It should be noted, however, that until 1958 Boganda remained firmly committed to the idea of assimilation and sought reform within the French empire rather than independence. Originally selected to run by the Catholic church hierarchy as a safe African candidate without leftist connections, Boganda remained, until his death, dependent on Europeans and French-speaking West Indians for advice and counsel. Born April 4, 1910, in Bobangui, a small forest village southwest of Bangui in the Lobaye basin, Boganda was a member of the Mbaka (Ngbaka) ethnic group whose ancestors had been linked in trade to the Bobangui slave trade hegemony. In 1901 Boganda's village had been introduced to European control through the far from gentle demands of a concessionary company, *Compagnie de Produits de la Lobaye,* which instituted a reign of terror in order to force the villagers to gather wild rubber under pain of beating and threats against family members. This state of affairs was scarcely interrupted by the three years of German control of the village from November 1911 through August 1914.

It is not surprising that the young Boganda responded to the kindness of the Holy Ghost Fathers who nursed him through smallpox, taught him to read, baptized him on Christmas Eve 1922, and set him on the path of learning that culminated in his ordination as the first Ubangian priest on March 17, 1938. What is surprising is how little the death of one of his kinsmen by whipping in Mbaïki, in November 1927, affected the young seminarian. Chief Mindogon was beaten to death by territorial guards because he had not furnished enough collectors of wild rubber for the *Compagnie Forestière Sangha-Oubangui.* One of Mindogon's sons, Jean-Bedel Bokassa, then six years old, was also to play an important role in Central African history. Familiar with both André Gide's *Voyage au Congo* and Albert Londre's *Terre d'Ebène,* Boganda had also read Marcel Homet's *Congo, Terre de Souffrance.* Yet these works did not stimulate Boganda's political awareness. He remained very much attached to France and was very slow to question the colonial regime. The brutal repression of the originally nonviolent protest movement of Karnu, a Gbaya religious figure, in December 1928 and the massacre on June 24, 1929, of the traditional leader Berondjoho, who had been hiding from colonial authorities in the forest between Bangui and Nola since 1909, initially seemed to have contributed little to Boganda's political awakening. Whatever his understanding of the message of liberation in the Gospel and the principles of the French Revolution, Boganda always seemed to have come to terms with the French. Once established as the leader of Ubangi, Boganda never really gave up the idea that a liberal democracy in close association with France was the preferred goal for Ubangi-Shari.

From the white settler viewpoint, of course, Boganda's rather naive attempts to introduce legislation against the forced production of cotton, racial segregation in public places, forced labor, and excessive head tax on poor cultivators during his first term as deputy to the National Assembly marked him as a radical. For his part, Boganda found that little of substance for the people of Ubangi-Shari could be accomplished in the French assembly. With little political or parliamentary experience, Boganda found in his first term that most French people were uninterested in African realities. He returned to Ubangi-Shari convinced that he would have to organize people from the grass roots up. Beginning in 1948 his championship of small African producers and his close ties with African teachers and truck drivers allowed him to develop his own base of political support. Yet the organization of African smallholders, which he created in 1948 with the collaboration of French advisers, Socoulolé (*Société Coopérative de l'Oubangui-Lobaye-Lessé*), proved to be an unmitigated disaster. Neither Boganda nor any of his followers had sufficient knowledge of production methods or management techniques to sustain the effort. Thwarted by the commercial monopolies with whom they were forced to deal and plagued by mismanagement. Socoulolé and a number of other transport and cooperative societies inspired by Boganda had very short lives. Boganda was absolved from an accusation of misappropriation of a 42.5 million CFA (*Colonies Françaises d'Afrique*) franc loan granted by the French government on December 1, 1947, but the whole movement had collapsed by 1951.

Boganda had cut himself off from all ties with French political parties upon his return to Ubangi-Shari in 1948 though he did marry a parliamentary secretary of the *Mouvement Républicain Populaire* (MRP), Michelle Jourdain, in 1950. It was this marriage to a French woman that marked his final rupture with the Catholic hierarchy and missionary establishment and left him free to create an autonomous African party with popular support.

On September 28, 1949, Boganda and a few other French-educated Ubangians founded the *Mouvement d'Evolution Sociale de l'Afrique Noire* (MESAN). The messianic implications of the acronym was a deliberate choice on Boganda's part. Under Boganda MESAN was never a political party in the usual sense of the term, but at once a quasi-religious movement and a rallying point for Ubangian self-identity and pride in response to white settler racism. Boganda even declared that MESAN was addressed to all blacks in the world. The black population of Bangui's poorer sections responded almost immediately to Boganda's call for equal rights. Black clerks refused to accept the familiar *tu* form of address, house servants no longer accepted being cuffed for minor offenses, and laborers resisted being lashed to force greater effort. As the movement spread into the countryside and reached even small villages, the European minority of Ubangi-Shari, racist for the most part, saw this change as revolutionary. During its first two years of existence MESAN had no clear structure or political goal. Like the *négritude* of Léopold Senghor, MESAN was simply a reaffirmation of black humanity. Well into the 1950s MESAN remained, for the mass of Ubangians, simply a symbol of resistance to white domination. In the MESAN appeals to the population in Sango, the local lingua franca, for the referendum on the Fifth Republic on September 28, 1958, their major message was still that blacks be accepted as full humans, and the independence MESAN called for was not African nationalism but a request for civil rights within the French community.

During 1950 and 1951 Boganda circulated throughout the countryside, speaking against the very real social, political, and economic injustices of the regime dominated by European colonialists. The more the European planters, miners, businessmen, missionaries, and government officials spoke against Boganda the more he became the hero of all black Central Africans. Finally in Bokanga, a small village in the Lobaye, on January 10, 1951, an incident occurred that brought Boganda's cooperative and political activities to a head. An altercation between a number of Portuguese traders and representatives of Socoulolé broke out as villagers protested price fixing by the Portuguese. Boganda and his French wife of scarcely a year, Michelle, were arrested by the French head of the Mbaïki District. They were held for forty-eight hours and on March 29 Boganda was condemned to two months in prison; his wife was given a fifteen-day sentence.

The news of their arrest and condemnation spread rapidly. Boganda immediately became the hero of the vast majority of Central Africans, many of whom had themselves suffered from arbitrary sentences and imprisonment. Though no longer a priest, Boganda became a messianic figure. Five months later Boganda was easily reelected to the Representative Council, and legal proceedings against him were dropped on March 30, 1952. MESAN won the majority of seats in the Ubangi-Shari Territorial Assembly. It now became clear to the more far-sighted members of the French government that African politicians like Boganda were no longer simply pawns and that the day of reckoning between reactionary settler control and legitimate demands of African citizens was fast approaching. As minister of Overseas France in 1951, François Mitterrand and his friends from the *Union Démocratique et Sociale de la Résistance* (UDSR) had helped African members to eliminate communist influence in the *Rassemblement Démocratique Africain* (RDA) so that this interterritorial party could now play a more active role in pressing for reform within the French Union. By 1953 the French colonial administration in general had begun to resist the overtly racist manifestations of the white settlers' cliques and accept the legitimacy of limited African political organization.

Toward the end of 1953 Boganda showed his goodwill toward the French administration by creating the biracial *Intergroupe Libéral Oubanguien* (ILO). Then in April 1954 a popular protest at Berbérati against the probable murder of a cook and his wife by a particularly vicious European public works agent led to a call to insurrection. This protest threatened to spread widely among the Gbaya who, present-day nationalists maintain, remembered the prophet Karnu. Governor Louis Sanmarco immediately sought Boganda's aid. Though Boganda had little support among the Gbaya, he accompanied Sanmarco to Berbérati and addressed the hostile crowd at the funeral of the couple, declaring that justice would henceforth be the same for blacks and whites. The crowd dispersed peacefully and the insurrection, which would have been bloodily crushed, was averted. Boganda had clearly demonstrated support beyond his forest base, and the French administration recognized this. Elected mayor of Bangui on November 18, 1956, and a few months later president of the Grand Council of AEF, Boganda was clearly the major political leader in both Ubangi-Shari and AEF.

Under the *Loi-Cadre* (Enabling Act) passed by the French assembly in 1956 and relative decrees, all of the territorial assemblies of the French Union were granted extended power. The creation of a territorial Council of Government, to which was transferred a considerable degree of the power and responsibility of AEF government, was also provided for. On March 31, 1957, MESAN obtained 347,000 out of 356,000 votes on an enlarged voter list and took all of the seats in the new Ubangi-Shari Territorial Assembly. When Boganda formed the first Council of Government as party leader under the French governor of Ubangi-Shari, Sanmarco, he was able to handpick his ministers. Boganda had Abel Goumba elected vice president as his most trusted MESAN supporter. This thirty-year-old French-educated medical assistant from Grimari in the central part of Ubangi-Shari had returned at Boganda's call to Ubangi-Shari in 1957 to be elected to the Territorial Assembly, having served in the French colonial service after his graduation. Unfortunately, Boganda also chose Roger Guérillot, a Frenchman who had rallied the colons to Boganda in the ILO, as minister of administrative affairs. Guérillot launched a drive to increase production that became simply a stricter application of the coffee and cotton monopolies. This proved to be a costly disaster that discredited MESAN in the eyes of the rural population. At the same time Guérillot persuaded Boganda to exclude a number of councillors from the eastern regions as communists due to their earlier allegiance to the RDA. Goumba resisted, and the council remained practically ineffective. Boganda, under attack by the French press and in despair, retreated on a long, private automobile tour of the country.

When the Algerian uprisings and de Gaulle's return to power on May 13, 1958, suddenly put independence on the horizon for Central Africa, Boganda was far from prepared to create an effective administration in Ubangi-Shari. Constitutional reforms since 1946 had somewhat weakened the centralized structure of French colonial administration and had given more authority to local bodies.

At the same time, the formation of political parties and the gradual extension of the franchise to the whole population had increased the African participation in their own government.

The constitution of 1958, creating the Fifth French Republic, provided for the free association of autonomous republics within the French Community, where France was envisaged as the senior partner. France would have jurisdiction over foreign policy, defense, currency, common economic and financial policy, policy on strategic raw materials, and, unless specifically excluded by agreement, over higher education, internal and external communications, and supervision of the courts. The president of the French republic was to be the president of the community's executive council made up of the prime ministers of the member states and the French ministers concerned with community affairs. A senate composed of members elected indirectly by each member state in proportion to its population and a common high court of arbitration was to complete the government. Ubangi-Shari, like every other member state, was to have its own government established by a separate constitution.

BOGANDA AND A UNIFIED CENTRAL AFRICA

Caught unprepared by the rapid turn of events, Boganda was aware that as a separate, landlocked state Ubangi-Shari would be an economic disaster. After a quick trip to Paris to see how serious the situation was, Boganda returned to Ubangi-Shari and on July 8, 1958, called for the total independence of Ubangi-Shari and all of Black Africa, perhaps trying to force de Gaulle's hand. The Ubangi-Shari assembly passed a motion to this effect on July 13. Then in the same month, Boganda sent Goumba and another of his close supporters, David Dacko, to meet with leaders of other territories who also opposed the breakup of French Africa into many weak states ruled over by France. Speaking directly to de Gaulle in Brazzaville in August, Boganda, as president of the Grand Council of AEF, publicly sought from the French president the option of a united AEF moving toward eventual independence rather than the balkanization of Africa demanded by the new constitution. De Gaulle answered that there were only two choices allowed for the referendum on September 28, 1958. Each territory was required either to accept the constitution and remain in the French Community or to reject it and be granted a separate independent status with no French assistance.

Boganda had little choice. He returned to Ubangi-Shari and announced that he would accept the French constitution, though reserving the right to independence at some later date. Boganda, in a last desperate bid to hold AEF together, proposed a grandiose scheme to join to it the territory between the Ubangi River and the Congo (Zaire) from the Belgian Congo. He proposed that AEF territories would, for a transition period, be autonomous under an alternating presidency that would rotate from Ubangian to Congolese, to Chadian, and finally to Gabonese leadership. This Central African Republic would form the nucleus of a United States of Latin Africa that would include Rwanda, Burundi, the rest of a liberated Belgian Congo, Angola, and Cameroon. Though the president of the Government Council in Moyen-Congo accepted the idea of unity, none of the other leaders wished to alienate France or give up their own power.

In Brazzaville on November 24, 1958, the delegates from Gabon, Chad, and Moyen-Congo declared the end of French Equatorial Africa and on December 1, 1958, a heavy-hearted Boganda proclaimed the constitution of a Central African Republic that included only the territory of the former French colony of Ubangi-Shari. His dreams of a unified state with a viable economic and political base were not realized, although he continued his efforts to maintain some regional unity into the early months of 1959. Even as he resigned himself to a much-truncated Central African Republic, Boganda took care to include in the constitution adopted in February the stipulation that the new state could give up part or even all of its sovereignty to a larger union.

THE DEATH OF A DREAM

With elections set for April 5, 1959, Boganda sought to gain all sixty legislative seats for his party with at least five seats reserved for French persons. On Easter, March 29, 1959, Boganda was killed in a yet unexplained airplane accident. Having booked passage on a regularly scheduled Union de Transport Aérien (UTA) flight from Berbérati to Bangui, Boganda's campaign and life were

The Boganda Monument in central Bangui. Photo courtesy of Thomas O'Toole.

ended in the Boda District on the left bank of the Lobaye in the smashed wreckage of an Atlas airplane. Though independence arrived in the Central African Republic on August 13, 1960, it came to a nation that had lost the only political leader who had emerged as a plausible national leader.[13]

NOTES

1. The best single source for the precolonial history of the Central African Republic is Dennis D. Cordell, "The Savanna Belt of North-Central Africa," in *History of Central Africa,* Vol. 1, ed. David Birmingham and Phyllis M. Martin, (London: Longman, 1983), 30–74.

2. Roger de Bayle des Hermens, *Recherches prehistoriques en République Centrafricaine* (Paris: Editions Labethno, 1973.

3. Pierre Vidal, *La civilisation mégalithique de Bouar: Prospections et fouilles,* 1962–1966 (Paris: Editions Labethno, 1969).

4. See the rather fanciful speculations of Pierre Kalck, *Histoire de la République Centrafricaine* (Paris: Editions Berger-Levrault, 1974), 50–58.

5. Cordell, "The Savanna Belt," 49–50.

6. See Robert W. Harms, *River of Wealth, River of Sorrow: The Central Zaire Basin in the Era of the Slave and Ivory Trade, 1500–1891* (New Haven: Yale University Press, 1981).

7. See Dennis D. Cordell, *Dar el-Kuti and the Last Years of the Trans-Saharan Slave-Trade*. Madison: University of Wisconsin Press, 1984.

8. See the documents gathered in Ghislain de Banville, *Ouaka 1900–1920* (Bambari, CAR: Centre Culturel Saint-Jean, 1983).

9. Thomas O'Toole, "The 1929–1931 Gbaya Insurrection in Ubangui-Shari: Messianic Movement or Village Self Defense?" *Canadian Journal of African Studies* 18 (1984) 329–344.

10. For a careful treatment of the health services and insight into French colonial rule in general, see Ralph A. Austen and Rita Headrick, "Equatorial Africa under Colonial Rule," in *History of Central Africa*, Vol. 2, ed. David Birmingham and Phyllis M. Martin, (London: Longman, 1983) 27–94.

11. See André Teulières, "Oubangui et France Libre," *Revue française d'études politiques Africaines* 117 (Sept. 1975) 55–72.

12. See the excellent biography of Boganda by Pierre Kalck, "Barthélemy Boganda: Tribun et visionnaire de l'Afrique centrale," in *Les Africains*, Vol. 3, ed. Charles-André Julien et al. (Paris: Editions Jeune Afrique, 1977) 103–137.

13. George Chafford, *Les carnets sêcrets de la dêcolonisation (Paris: Berger-Levrault, 1967)*, 171.

3

The Central African Polity

BOGANDA TO DACKO

Had anyone been asked early in 1959 to put together a "worse case scenario" for the history of the first thirty years of the Central African Republic, one might have imagined something close to the actual sequence of events that has unfolded in this archetypical, neocolonial polity that has yet to become an autonomous state.[1] To speak of "ambiguity" as some have done to characterize the French role in the Central African Republic is only to use a euphemism for what must be seen as a fiasco, the consequences of which have yet to be fully appreciated. The record speaks for itself: France's continued military involvement, though supplemented by massive injections of economic and financial aid, have utterly failed to stabilize its client state.

Although there can be no question that, in the words of a knowledgeable observer, "France has had a large share of the blame for what has happened in the Central African Republic," to cast France in the role of the villain in a kind of morality play is hardly illuminating. If villains must be identified, they can be found in large numbers among Central African officials irrespective of regional or ethnic affiliations as well as among neighboring states. Furthermore, among the sins of omission and commission attributable to the French, perhaps the more consequential are traceable to the colonial period, long before French troops were called upon to redeem, in their own very special ways, the errors of the past. The gratuitous burning of villages and killing of people that occurred during the so-called Gbaya uprising of 1929–1931, the arbitrary humiliations of village notables that occurred repeatedly during the first and second decades of this century, and the more or less systematic application of force from the center as a substitute for autonomous local political development are recurrent themes in the history of the Central African Republic. No attempt to understand the confused and fractious nature of the Central African political environment can ignore this historical backdrop.

To find one's way through the complexities of the Central African labyrinth one must give full weight to the expansion of the French national interest to include the interest of specific Central African factions to the exclusion of others. What is unique about the case of the CAR is the extent to which this process of selective identification has been influenced by forces operating outside the state's geographical boundaries. Political developments in Chad, Congo, Gabon, Libya, Zaire, and even farther afield have had a determining impact on the way in which the French came to define their friends and enemies within the Central African arena. Though Boganda's charismatic leadership had at first frightened both the colonial administration and the local French residents, most of the latter had come to see his vague African unity and black pride stance as far less threatening than even the by then largely quite acceptable RDA to which Goumba had been attracted.

With Boganda's death the elections for the National Legislative Assembly scheduled for April 5, 1959, were of little consequence to most Africans. Only 55 percent of the eligible voters participated in electing Boganda's hand-picked candidates to the fifty-five African seats in the sixty-person legislature. The interim head of government, Abel Goumba, as former president of the Council of Government and minister of state, seemed virtually assured the presidency of the new nation. This was not to be the case. With the backing of the French high commissioner, the European-dominated Chamber of Commerce, and Boganda's French widow, David Dacko, a relative of Boganda, who had served under him as minister of the interior and later minister of economic affairs, was chosen instead. Goumba was perceived as too nationalistic by the French. Without Boganda the assembly was easily swayed by the united European nucleus, which supported the more malleable Dacko. At the first meeting in May Dacko ignored the parliamentary constitution that had been granted by the French and took complete control of the government. In July, Dacko discharged Goumba, who was still serving as minister of finance and planning. The twenty-nine-year-old former schoolteacher, David Dacko, became the sole leader of the Central African Republic in spite of the fact that he had virtually no popular support. On October 3, 1959, a motion of censure requiring a two-thirds vote according to the constitution was put forth by Pierre Maleombho, president of the legislative assembly. When it looked as if the vote would succeed, Dacko used trucks and money supplied by his European supporters to recruit and transport members of his Mbaka ethnic group from the Lobaye area to surround the assembly. Claiming that the censure motion was a movement against the memory of Boganda by his enemies, Dacko was able to utilize his kinship ties to Boganda as a rallying point for a limited and contrived "popular" uprising. This pressure and a number of well-placed bribes caused the censure motion to fail. In May 1960 Dacko arbitrarily replaced Maleombho as head of the assembly; Dacko named his friend, Michel Adama-Tambou, to the post.

While Dacko was consolidating his power at home, he was also trying to preserve some semblance of Boganda's larger union with Chad, Congo, and Gabon. By July 1960 French opposition and political and economic forces within each of the four former AEF member states had virtually eliminated any possibility of a viable federation. The French had never overcome the difficulties of integrating physically or economically the vast territory they had placed under one governor-general in Brazzaville. The postwar political reforms had discouraged AEF-wide political parties. The African leadership in Gabon, for example, desired to be rid of the poorer colonies. Some political leaders in Brazzaville feared that Dacko, like Boganda, wished to reincorporate members of the Mbaka ethnic community in the northern part of Moyen-Congo into the Central African Republic. In Chad northern Muslims feared their increased minority status in a larger non-Muslim federation. The AEF could not survive the centrifugal forces. In Bangui on August 13, 1960, André Malraux, in the name of the French government, signed the independence agreement in the presence of Yvon Bourges, the French *haut-commissaire général* of AEF and Paul Bordier, the *haut-commissaire* in Bangui. On Sunday,

August 14, a hastily called assembly named Dacko acting head of state until a president could be chosen.

Faced with the rapid and largely unplanned independence movement that would deliver the government of the new state into the hands of a small group of French-backed opportunists, Abel Goumba and a few other farsighted MESAN members had created an opposition party, the *Mouvement d'Evolution Démocratique de l'Afrique Centrale* (MEDAC) in May. Goumba and his followers sought open negotiations, as promised by the French constitution, to determine the form of government to be established for the Central African Republic and the nature of the relationship of this government with France. In reply Dacko improvised a rump MESAN congress and had himself named head of MESAN, declaring himself to be Boganda's successor. Reassured by the presence of French administrators and technicians in every post of importance, by the backing of French colons, miners, and businessmen who felt they would control him, Dacko proceeded rapidly to consolidate his power.

To test his electoral strength Dacko held an election to fill the seats vacated by the deaths of Boganda and his colleague, Albert Fagama, eighteen months earlier. On September 20, in spite of tremendous pressure from Dacko and the French circles in Bangui, MEDAC received 20 percent of the eligible vote. It was clear to Dacko and his French advisors that free national elections might result in the election of a government far less susceptible to French control. Still hoping to achieve a compromise, Goumba accepted a place on a constitutional committee overseen by a French legal advisor. Here Goumba judiciously counseled that the minimum age for the presidency be set at forty, thereby eliminating both himself and Dacko from the competition. Dacko and his French-dominated clique realized that the recommendation of the constitutional committee would pose a threat to their position, and on November 12 Dacko called on the assembly simply to confirm him and themselves in power with neither an election nor a constitutional referendum. At the same time he requested and received broad powers to suppress opposition parties and groups, to arrest potential subversives, and to jail opponents he judged dangerous to public order. MEDAC called for peaceful demonstrations against these, in their view, dangerous precedents.

Goumba's suggestion that Dacko was simply an agent of French policy had clearly struck home to the more politically aware urban population. When Dacko accused the MEDAC deputies in the assembly of fomenting tribalism, they walked out in silent protest.

Dacko responded swiftly. Staging an incident with the French high commissioner, Governor Paul Bordier, Dacko made a show of breaking relations with France to draw the attention of Central Africans away from his own undemocratic behavior. Supported by leaders from the other former French colonies and, in retrospect, clearly backed by his French councillors, Dacko seized power. On December 23 Dacko's ministers pronounced the dissolution of MEDAC and a French magistrate in Dacko's serivce called upon the assembly to abolish Goumba's parliamentary immunity. On Christmas Eve the assembly did so. An hour later French-directed gendarmes arrested Goumba for provoking disorder by questioning Dacko's arbitrary seizure of power. Seven other MEDAC deputies were arrested on December 29 for the same offense; on December 30 Dacko declared the assembly purged. During his New Year's Eve radio broadcast Colonel Roger Barberat, the French government's representative in Bangui, called upon all French citizens living in the Central African Republic to give Dacko's government their support.

GOVERNMENT UNDER DACKO

From the French perspective an independent Central African Republic under Dacko was the best arrangement possible in face of the rapid collapse of the Franco-African *Communauté.*[2] An accommodating client, Dacko, had accepted without question bilateral cooperation agreements that, despite subsequent revisions, still provide the essential foundation of France's ubiquitous influence in the affairs of the Republic. These agreements covered precisely those areas of jurisdiction that had been reserved for France under the 1958 constitution, i.e., external relations, defense, currency, international trade and finance, strategic raw materials, judicial review, higher education, long distance transportation, and telecommunications. Those areas of sovereignty that the French government had explicitly retained for itself in 1958 through its dominant position in the community were once more deposited in French hands for safeguarding by the bilateral cooperative agreements Dacko accepted. For the French this system of structured "cooperation" linkages with the CAR institutionalized and routinized continued French presence and involvement in the political and economic processes of the country. A substantial majority of senior managerial positions both in the government and in the private sector remained staffed by French nationals.

Dacko's role, despite rhetoric to the contrary, was simply to retain political power in order to give some legitimacy to this neocolonial state of affairs. In this regard the first year of Dacko's regime was a disaster. A dual system of administration with French assistance and poorly trained Central Africans at all levels scarcely functioned. Roads went without repair, cotton production declined, and only the presence of the French army preserved order. Offices multiplied rapidly as more and more Central Africans and their French advisers sought lucrative positions. High salaries were offered to French typists and secretaries to induce them to come to the Central African Republic. By 1962 the situation was critical: Both Central African ministers and officials and their French shadows went on an orgy of spending—attending conferences abroad, driving luxury cars, and purchasing equipment with reckless abandon. To compound the difficulties, international speculators flowed in to reap their own benefits. The uncontrolled rush of Central African farmers and laborers to the diamond areas disrupted coffee and cotton production. French and other profiteers in collusion with CAR officials made large sums but, given the administrative state of affairs, little revenue accrued to the national treasury. Profiteering by officials in all areas of the economy was so rampant that even Dacko ultimately became upset, declaring to the assembly on October 2, 1962, that the Sango expression *mbi yeke gi kobe ti yanga ti mbi* (I search for food for my own mouth) must give way to a sense of public service.

Democratic forms of government under Dacko were an illusion. Laws were proposed by his French advisers and passed without modification by the assembly. In December 1962 the assembly was called into session by Dacko to pass a constitutional amendment to limit its own powers and on November 15, 1963, he, in total disregard of the constitution, asked the assembly to prolong the presidential term in office to seven years and grant the office more power. Ultimately the shame of parliamentary government gave way to naked force. In June 1961 Dacko had MESAN youth leaders who criticized continued French control arrested. On February 22, 1962, a Supreme Court, still composed of French magistrates, condemned Goumba and two other MEDAC officials to life imprisonment.[3] At Bambari, from July 28 to August 1, 1962, Dacko staged a meeting of some 500 delegates. He declared MESAN would henceforth be a mass party to which every Central African—man, woman, and child—would pay dues and that this unified party would be the means by which the whole Central African people would have a voice in government.

By January 5, 1964, when MESAN, totally dominated by Dacko and his supporters, presented him as the sole candidate for a seven-year term as president, the conclusion was foregone. He was elected by 100 percent of those who voted. Few were brave enough to question the fact of restricted access to the polls. The election of Dacko's sixty hand-picked MESAN candidates to the assembly on March 19, 1964, was also quietly accepted.

In effect this election marked the end of any overt political opposition to Dacko in the Central African Republic. Dacko thereafter turned his attention to the pressing economic needs of the country. He seemed to realize that the predatory import-export economy that had functioned under colonial rule would have to be modified. He made a number of attempts to achieve some participation by the Central African government in cotton and diamond production. In 1964, with the technical and financial support of the French government, he established a number of small processing industries, including a milk and cheese factory at Sarbi, a brick and pottery works in Bangui, and a small plastics fabrication plant near Bangui.

Throughout 1964 and 1965 he had even more grandiose plans in mind. Though many of them—a proposed railroad link through Cameroon, the Bakouma uranium mines, and ironworks to process ore from Bogoin—never got off the drawing board, some were realized. Dacko negotiated a revitalization of the textile factory at Boali in spite of opposition by French business interests. He also obtained General de Gaulle's promise to construct the Bangui-M'Poko international airport. Relying completely on external technical assistance, a number of forestry and cattle-keeping projects showed some promise in these years. In December 1964 Dacko presided over the signing of a formal agreement creating the *Union Douanière et Economique de l'Afrique Centrale* (UDEAC), a common market made up of the Central African Republic, Chad, Congo, Gabon, and Cameroon, with its main offices in Bangui.

In spite of overwhelming odds, the number of students in school doubled between October 1959 and October 1965, though virtually all secondary teachers remained French because little provision had been made to train African teachers. Attempting to fill administrative positions with Central Africans in a short period of time, Dacko was forced to draw heavily on former and potential teachers, thereby exacerbating the deficit of the country's educational system. In the health sector, the situation was even worse. Although spending in this sector doubled from 1959 to 1965, the level and availability of even rudimentary health care for most Central Africans declined precipitously, as poor management, lack of professionalism, and gross corruption took their toll. Rural infirmaries had neither medications nor personnel and the risk of a major epidemic grew extremely high.

Dacko's foreign policy never exhibited much coherence. Speaking in favor of African unity even before the founding of the Organization of African Unity (OAU) in 1963, Dacko nevertheless remained closely tied to French assistance. On May 19, 1964, Dacko signed an agreement of cooperation with Nationalist China, and then on August 27 of the same year recognized the People's Republic of China as "the sole representative of the Chinese people" while a Central African delegation was still in Taiwan. In November 1964 he spoke forcefully against Belgian and U.S. intervention in the former Belgian Congo, yet in July 1964 he complained that the withdrawal of French troops from the CAR was premature and in February 1964 applauded the intervention of French paratroopers in Gabon.

In May 1964 Dacko's sudden decision to take an imposing delegation on a forty-nine-day tour of most of the capitals of Western Europe can only be understood as his last desperate attempt to find some solution to the consequence of political misrule and the economic collapse facing his country. Doubling direct taxes and tripling others in 1962 had had little effect on the spiraling national debt. Faced with a treasury bled dry by poor management, theft, and diminished revenues, in January 1965 Dacko doubled the head tax and reestablished the "donated" labor of colonial times, but to no avail.

In November 1965 when the Chinese ambassador refused to pay promised aid in cash rather than in kind, bankruptcy loomed. In early December 1965 a defeated Dacko offered his resignation to his ministers, who refused to accept it. Faced with the threat of a general strike called by the head of the state union, Maurice Gouandjia (Abel Goumba's cousin), the French planned to stage a coup d'état in order to install a government of their own choosing and avoid the possibility of a leftist outcome such as had occurred in Congo-Brazzaville in 1963. The new head of state was to be Commander Jean Izamo, the head of the gendarmerie, whom the French government considered safe. Events of the evening of December 31, 1965, and the early morning hours of January 1, 1966, changed these carefully laid plans.[4]

THE BOKASSA INTERLUDE

The unexpected intervention of a forty-four-year-old Mbaka army officer, Jean-Bedel Bokassa, who claimed to be Boganda's nephew, took Bangui and the French by surprise.[5] A member of the French army since 1939, Bokassa had seen service in Indochina, leaving the French army with the rank of lieutenant in 1960. He had returned to Bangui to form Dacko's war cabinet. In 1963, by then a major, Bokassa had his contacts within the French military pressure Dacko into appointing him chief of staff in the Ministry of Defense. On New Year's Eve 1965 Bokassa, by then a colonel, turned down Izamo's invitation to a cocktail party. Bokassa felt that Dacko had sold out in favor of the gendarmerie. Bokassa had been alerted that he was to be arrested, if not assassinated by those plotting the forthcoming coup d'état. Instead, he suggested that Izamo follow Dacko's advice and avoid the "colonial" practice of celebrating New Year's Eve while the Central African people lived in poverty. Bokassa asked Izamo to stop by the military camp at Roux to sign some end-of-year inventories. To allay suspicion of his own impending coup, Izamo went to the camp at about 7:00 P.M. only to be arrested by Bokassa.

At 11:00 P.M., according to a careful plan developed by one of Bokassa's trusted aides, Captain Alexandre Banza, Bokassa ordered the army to occupy the administrative center of town and subdue the gendarmerie. Led by young officers, veterans of Indochina like Bokassa, the army seized the airport to forestall any possibility that the French would send in troops to support Izamo, their choice as Dacko's replacement. In the meantime, Dacko, playing out his role in the French-directed charade, was preparing for the Izamo coup. Early in the evening of December 31, 1965, Dacko discharged his servants, burned his personal papers, and went out to dinner. When minor fighting broke out around the ministerial villas, Dacko fled in his automobile toward his home region southwest of Bangui. Captured by Bokassa's forces, Dacko bowed to the inevitable and on January 1, 1966, at 3:20 A.M. turned the government over to Bokassa, who declared that he had intervened to save Dacko's life and prevent a "pro-Chinese" coup by Izamo. Rather than reveal its own machinations, the French government remained neutral.

During the night of January 2 and the early morning of January 3, 1966, Bokassa hastily created a "revolutionary council" to lead the new government. On January 4 Bokassa had Dacko's legal advisor draft a pair of documents under which he would rule. According to these sketchy articles the constitution of November 20, 1964, was abolished as were the National Assembly, the Constitutional Council, and the Economic and Social Council. Bokassa was at once president and minister of defense, information, and justice. Banza, the intellectual organizer of the New Year's Eve coup, was promoted to the rank of lieutenant colonel and made minister of finance. Since Banza was a Gbaya, a large ethnic group whose members had been excluded from government circles under Dacko, this and other astute appointments, such as a young civil servant from the northwestern part of the country, Ange Patassé, as minister of development, gained Bokassa considerable popular support. Bokassa let his ministers assume full responsibility for their departments during the first six months of 1966, and considerable progress in reorganization and better management was made in some areas. Bokassa did, however, reserve the right to make all government decisions without consulting an assembly and with only superficial consultation with his own appointed

Council of Ministers. Bokassa assumed the functions of president of MESAN and placed the army in charge of a number of public services.

In the early months of his regime, Bokassa maintained his residence in the military camp and may well have intended to step down in favor of a civilian government once he had reformed the administrative and economic chaos that prevailed in the country. Although Bokassa came to power by means of a military-based, palace coup, his regime began with a substantial degree of public support. Many of his decisions in the early months directly improved the lives of the majority of the country's citizens. He started construction of a large concrete central market in Bangui, to establish a public transport system, ordered buses from France, donated his first month's salary as president to the main hospital in Bangui, subsidized two national dance orchestras, and paid in cash the debts that Central African butchers owed Chadian cattle-breeders so that meat would be available once more in the markets. Such acts, though seemingly unimportant to outsiders, did create for the first time the sense for most Central Africans that the government could actually act in their interests.

In foreign affairs the regime gained support much more slowly.[6] General de Gaulle's government was reluctant to embrace a military leader who had assumed the mantle of authority on his own. Relations with France were not completely regular until Jean Herly, a former colonial administrator, was appointed French ambassador to Bangui in August 1966 and Bokassa was received in Paris by de Gaulle in November 1966. Throughout the love-hate relationship between the French government and Bokassa, the Central African leader continued to maintain his French citizenship. By September 1967 Bokassa was so obsessed by the fear of plots that he made a trip to Paris to ask the French government to grant him the protection of French troops. On November 10, eighty French parachutists of the Eleventh Division arrived. This number was to grow in the next year until French troops represented almost 20 percent of the military force in the country by 1969. Yet Bokassa made a short-lived attempt to bolt the franc zone in February and March of 1966 and establish a *Union des Etats de l'Afrique Centrale* (UEAC) composed of Chad, Zaire, and the Central African Republic, with its own currency.

In the long run Bokassa was as unsuccessful as Dacko in solving the administrative and economic problems facing the country. Bokassa had little success in eliminating France's neocolonial control over the Central African Republic. Both as a client and as a supplier, France remained far and away the leading trade partner for the CAR. In 1968, 42 percent of the exports from the Central African Republic went to France. By 1978 this had grown to 63 percent. Imports to the Republic from France represented 61 percent of all goods imported in 1968 and were still at 58 percent in 1978. French government aid to Bokassa's regime reflected a continued willingness to use public funds to preserve and foster economic, cultural, and political conditions favorable to the development of French private interests. As a rule, bilateral aid is generally regarded as tied to the furthering of the donor's national interest and more susceptible to being used for political leverage than multilateral aid. From 1970 through 1979 France's development aid to the Central African Republic averaged about 87 percent bilateral assistance. France not only allocated a much higher share of its aid than other noncommunist assistance-granting countries to bilateral programs, but it also devoted a larger portion of that bilateral assistance to technical cooperation programs, most of it in the form of very high remuneration paid to French technical assistance personnel, especially secondary and university teachers. Almost totally reliant upon French support in both the public and private sectors, the CAR under Bokassa remained a French colony in all but name.

Bokassa had little success in eliminating the internal causes of corruption and malfeasance in public and private life. He brought charges against only a few selected officials of Dacko's government for theft and embezzlement. Furthermore, Bokassa had to reward the army for helping him to power. Officers received promotions and increases in salary while deficits mounted, and the cost of imported consumer goods rose while productive investments declined.

As minister of finance, Lieutenant Colonel Alexandre Banza, the regime's strong man, actually attempted to fight rampant government corruption, but by the end of the regime's first year, Banza was eased out of power. On April 12, 1969, Bokassa had him brutally tortured and executed on the charge of plotting against the government. Without Banza the distinction between Bokassa's personal accounts and those of the state ceased to exist. Central Africa gradually became Bokassa's private business and the president-for-life (after March 1972) publicly carried on a trade in diamonds and other commodities. By and large, though, this "privatization" of state revenues proved quite satisfactory to the dominant French interests, and Bokassa was able to welcome his "dear cousin" Valéry Giscard d'Estaing, the president of the Fifth French Republic, to Bangui on an official state visit in March 1975.

By 1967 it was clear that Bokassa was not moving toward early elections. The few ministers in the government were appointed, revoked, and even executed at his will. The assembly and MESAN officials were dismissed at will. The administration created by the colonial regime continued to disintegrate. Only a handful of the 4,000 Central African government officials and agents played any part in political life. CAR politics was increasingly the domain of a small bureaucratic bourgeoisie that occupied the former colonial offices and villas and mimicked the colonial administration as best they could. The majority of the people of the Central African Republic lived their lives with little or no concern for this charade. The fact that France still controlled the currency prevented total bankruptcy. Internal disorder was kept in check somewhat by restrictions placed by France on the national budget, which, it should be remembered, was less than the working capital of any large Parisian store.

Limited as the spoils of government were, they were virtually the only game in town for the Central African bureaucratic bourgeoisie. Private capital and the means of production were almost entirely in the hands of a small foreign entrepreneurial class. The primary economic activities of the country involved exports and were dominated by foreign-controlled monopolies working the diamond mines, timber concessions, and plantation agriculture as well as most wholesale and retail businesses. Assuring his control of the state and "privatizing" the state revenues became an obsession with Bokassa and his supporters in the early 1970s. This situation, in turn, produced gaping deficiencies in the effective provisions of public goods and services. Ultimately, attempts were made by elements of the bureaucratic bourgeoisie who were not in his inner circle to replace Bokassa. In December 1974, August

1975, and finally in February 1976, serious attempts by opponents within the army and the gendarmerie occurred and failed. These and many other plots, real or imagined, made a strong impression on Bokassa. His response, though, was unexpected. Long an admirer of the French military tradition and especially of Napoleon I, Bokassa declared on December 4, 1976, that the Central African Republic would become the Central African Empire. Bokassa proclaimed himself emperor, established a hereditary succession, promulgated a new constitution, and created an imperial court at Berengo near his home village of Bobangui in the Lobaye. A year later the world witnessed the bizarre pomp of the imperial coronation of Bokassa I and his wife Catherine in Bangui.

The ceremony, which cost a third of the national revenue for the year, proved the final blow to an already faltering economy. In July 1978, Ange Patassé, the head of government since September 1976, stepped down in favor of Henri Maidou, who had been serving as minister of education, but neither could do anything to solve the economic crisis. In December 1978 the eccentricities of the emperor were further revealed by the enormous public sums he lavished on the celebration of the first anniversary of the coronation. Consequently, the government was unable to pay student stipends and civil service salaries at the end of November and December.

By January 1979 the situation was acute. The emperor ordered all lycée students to purchase uniforms fabricated by an establishment owned by his wife. When some students were turned away from class for not wearing the required uniform on January 18, 1979, they staged a demonstration. The cries "down with the uniforms" soon became "down with Bokassa." By January 19 widespread looting of stores in the center of town raged unchecked. That night the army moved into a section of town inhabited largely by Banda and Sara ethnic groups, historical enemies of Bokassa's own Mbaka ethnic group, and a number of violent encounters resulted. Some 150 to 200 deaths occurred, mostly lycée students but also younger children and a number of women.

Bokassa responded with a radio address in which he blamed both Soviet and Libyan intervention as the cause of the unrest and stated that as emperor he would abolish the government's order in regard to the wearing of uniforms. With supplementary aid from the French he then paid the student stipends and civil servant salaries, with raises of more than 50 percent, and relative peace was restored. The realization, however, that street demonstrations could have an effect was not forgotten.

Political opposition soon began to manifest itself. Tracts denouncing Bokassa's riches began to circulate widely in the capital, and on April 17 a number of teachers and students were arrested on suspicion of being the originators of these tracts. Two days later a general strike began at the university and the lycées. On April 12 the army began a ten-day occupation of the university and by April 17 and 18 clandestine student meetings were being held all around Bangui. On April 18, 19, and 20, students and young people in many of the *kodros*[7] were subjected to a brutal roundup organized by the army and the Imperial Guard. At least 100 young people were then beaten to death at Ngaragba prison in the presence of, and probably with the participation of, Bokassa himself. By April 22 and 23 their deaths and secret burials were common knowledge throughout the city.

In mid-May when Amnesty International made this massacre public, the French people began to question severely their government's support for Bokassa. Despite France's many strategic, political, and economic interests in the country, Bokassa had become an embarrassment. During the Sixth Franco-African Congress in Kigali, Rwanda, May 20–22, the French delegation noted that the Central African ambassador to France had resigned in protest of the prison massacre. The French delegation then sought and obtained the creation of an African Mission of Inquiry consisting of magistrates from the Ivory Coast, Liberia, Rwanda, Senegal, and Togo to go to Bangui to look into the affair. President Giscard d'Estaing presented a strong front by suspending military aid to the Central African Empire, awaiting the report of this mission of inquiry. The act was largely symbolic because France has ceased giving military aid to Bokassa sometime earlier.

By July 1979 a number of very different opposition groups existed outside the country. The four main ones were: (1) the *Association Nationale des Etudiants Centrafricains* (ANECA), composed of students who had fled to Brazzaville after the April crackdown; (2) the *Front Patriotique Oubanguien* (FPO) directed by Abel Goumba, the only major opponent who had never participated in power under Bokassa, at the time serving in Cotonou, Benin, with the World Health Organization; (3) the *Mouvement de Libération du Peuple Centrafricain* (MLPC), created by Ange Patassé in Paris; and (4) finally the *Front de Libération des Oubanguiens* (FLO), founded by the former Central African ambassador in Paris, Sylvestre Bangui, after a spectacular protest resignation. Personality and political differences, though, kept these and other Central African opponents of Bokassa's increasingly megalomaniacal and barbarous rule from becoming an effective counterforce.

In the meantime the French government was doing all it could to find a way to make Bokassa step down before the African Mission of Inquiry established that the head of a government to which France had given so much support was personally guilty of a mass killing. President Bongo of Gabon was asked to arrange a meeting between René Journiac, a representative of the French government, and Emperor Bokassa in Franceville, Gabon, on August 1, 1979. Bokassa refused to attend and declined the invitation to resign.

On August 16 the report of the mission of inquiry appeared in Dakar confirming the Amnesty International reports and concluding with "quasi-certainty" that Bokassa had personally participated in the Ngaragba prison massacres. The following day the French government announced the cessation of all but the most necessary health, education, and food support to the Central African Empire, while at the same time completing plans for an "Operation Barracuda," a French military intervention. On the night of September 20 and the morning of September 21, with David Dacko as a symbol of Central African participation, a French military detachment arrived in Bangui to "re-establish the republic." Since Bokassa was conveniently absent seeking aid in Libya, the coup was peaceful, and on September 26, 1979, David Dacko established a new government. Dacko again assumed the post of president and retained Henri Maidou, Bokassa's head of state, as vice president. He made Sylvestre Bangui his minister of foreign affairs but found no place for Goumba or Patassé in his new government.

Bokassa in the meantime having been refused entry into France in spite of his French passport, found political exile in the Ivory Coast. The Houphouet-Boigny regime claimed to accept

Abandoned statue of Bokassa at his Berengo palace. Photo courtesy of Thomas O'Toole.

Bokassa solely out of "Christian charity," but the action certainly had the effect of assisting the French government out of a very embarrassing impasse.

DACKO ENCORE

During the fourteen years of Jean-Bedel Bokassa's rule—first as president, then as emperor—the basic conditions for accomplishing national development were by no means met. Instead of evolving a public character, the state was almost completely privatized by Bokassa and his handful of supporters. Instead of stimulating productivity, the state bureaucracy incarnated nonproductivity and indeed counterproductivity; the state was bankrupt. Instead of some measure of national independence being attained, dependence on France had grown. Instead of providing for the basic needs of the Central African people, the bureaucratic bourgeoisie had reduced this already poor country to conditions of abject mendicancy and impoverishment so extreme that mere survival had become the average citizen's daily struggle in the face of repression and scarcity. Dacko's immediate task upon reassuming power in September 1979 was to establish a bureaucracy capable of carrying out routine daily functions of government. Given the fewer than one hundred trained and prepared managerial personnel available in the country, it was inevitable that Dacko's first cabinet retain a good number of people who had been involved with the Bokassa regime. It was almost as inevitable that the conspicuous consumption of this elite would be upsetting to the urban lumpen proletariat that had continued to swell the shantytowns on Bangui's periphery during the Bokassa years.

The key factor in Dacko's relative success during the first six months of his return was the solid French backing he received. Dacko received some US $17 million in assistance from France during this period, and French troops remained a visible sign of support. In order to remove any incriminating evidence of the links between Bokassa, President Giscard d'Estaing, and other members of his government, several French officials in Bangui moved rapidly to transport all of Bokassa's papers to safekeeping in France. At considerable expense the French had new legal currency printed for the country, replacing Bokassa's visage with that of a more neutral buffalo.

Most other potential aid donors were reluctant to rush to the aid of Dacko as France's surrogate ruler in this poor, landlocked country. Even with the reactivation of the French garrison at Bouar it took considerable persuasion before the European Economic Community tentatively agreed to go ahead with a $20 million aid package consisting of loans and subsidies. Much of this assistance and virtually all other possible aid were to be directed toward increasing agricultural production and to infrastructural development at basic levels. Coffee and cotton exports had fallen sharply during the Bokassa years and even the diamond-mining industry, which accounted for 50 percent of the nation's export earnings, had declined.

Unfortunately, rather than addressing the underlying economic problems confronting the country, Dacko was far more preoccupied in the first year of his return to office with consolidating his personal power. With French assistance Dacko was able by November 1979 to crush the initially strong opposition of Ange Patassé, who, as an outspoken critic of continued French domination, rallied the support of lycée students and unemployed young in Fou and Muskine, two of the shantytowns on Bangui's periphery. In order to draw attention away from the fact that Bokassa had named Dacko as his personal counselor in 1976, Dacko held a series of public trials of other former Bokassa accomplices. These trials took place in Bangui's main sports stadium early in 1980. Broadcast over the radio, they provided an arena for Central Africans to express hatred toward the Bokassa regime while giving the Dacko government an appearance of credibility and order. Though skeptical, most urban Central Africans followed these trials very carefully, and their staging did lend some popular support to Dacko's government.

The first year of Dacko's return to power was marked by a number of strikes in various sectors, sporadic attacks on government officials, and growing unrest among disaffected teachers and students as well as among the urban dispossessed. But most of this activity took the form of unorganized, spontaneous reaction to delays in pay or other mistakes of a generally unresponsive government. Dacko weathered the difficulties by a judicious application of police action and economic and political persuasion. With the help of the French, Dacko was able to meet fairly regularly the government's bloated payroll and to continue to enlarge student scholarships, thereby easing tensions within the civil service and at the university and lycées in Bangui.

Following the suggestions of his French advisers, Dacko initially made little attempt to upset the status quo. He chose, rather, to continue a government based upon the same small group of Francophiles from the ethnic groups established for generations on the banks of the Ubangi River. Virtually all of this clique had shared power since 1960 whether under Dacko or Bokassa. In February Dacko created his own party, the *Union Démocratique Centrafricaine* (UDC), which he claimed was born from the ashes of Boganda's MESAN party. A party in name only, UDC was officially inaugurated during the course of a carefully staged party congress in March 1980, which passed a series of grandiose and sterile resolutions ranging from support for world disarmament to promises of great strides toward economic development for the country. Immediate results were insubstantial and most observers acknowledged that the UDC was little more than another feeble attempt to legitimatize Dacko's rule.

Unfortunately for Dacko such window dressing could not overcome the naked fact that the French military patrolled the streets of Bangui and a personal bodyguard of French troops guarded him at all times. The more politically aware segments of the population, especially the students, teachers, and employed workers in Bangui, increased their demands for the removal of former Bokassa supporters at all levels of government as a step toward a less French-dominated system. At the same time ever-mounting inflation and food sabotages compounded the frustrations of people throughout the country but especially the urban under- and unemployed who could not resort to subsistence food growing. The French government, moreover, was faced with strong political pressures at home to reduce support for its puppet regime in Bangui. The French pressured Dacko into reducing government jobs, army promotions, and student financial aid in order to balance the budget. Given Dacko's tenuous control of affairs these economically sound moves proved politically dangerous. On April 9 and 10, 1980, students returning from Easter vacation were greeted by the news that only those with excellent grades would henceforth receive governmental financial support. Given the poor quality of education, the lack of books and materials, and the general decline in scholastic standards during the final years of Bokassa's rule, this posed a threat to the hundreds of young people whose livelihood and that of their families depended on their status as subsidized students. Consequently student strikes erupted in Bangui and in a few of the larger regional towns.

Finally in June 1980, clashes broke out between government gendarmes and rural populations in the Ouham and Ouham-Pendé regions over supposed food levies applied by UDC officials. On June 25 university and lycée students again began demonstrations. For most students, the cause was simply to reverse their probably justifiably low grades and *baccalauréat* failures, but a growing resistance to French domination of education and other aspects of Central African life was again voiced. Obviously, large numbers of Central Africans wished for a more independent government than that which the French had put in power on September 21, 1979.

For their part the French were upset that Dacko did not seem able to control affairs to their satisfaction. Scarcely a week had gone by since he was placed in power without a strike or a work stoppage, and French business interests were beginning to voice their concern. Faced with the real possibility that the French might withdraw their support for him, Dacko proved more tenacious than his previous record would have suggested. On July 9, Dacko dissolved the government of "public safety" under which he was ruling and forced the hands of Prime Minister Bernard-Christian Ayandho and Vice President Henri Maidou. On July 18 Maidou declared his intention to run for president under the new constitution that was expected to be presented to the Central African people in early 1981. A few days later he declared that he had asked the French to intervene against Bokassa and then voiced his support for a multiparty state. On August 10 Ayandho also affirmed that he had worked secretly against Bokassa and would seek election on his own right. Both Maidou and Ayandho expected that the French would swing to their support as a means of reducing the obvious embarrassment the French government faced by continued support of Dacko. Dacko moved rapidly to counter their attempts. Dacko evicted both Maidou and Ayandho from office and placed them under house arrest on August 23. Dacko explained that these actions were necessary in order to preserve order on the eve of a major labor rally because of the manifest unpopularity of these two former officials in the Bokassa government. By early September public demonstrations and continued labor and students unrest led Dacko to attempt to defuse the growing dissatisfaction with his regime by having his minister of justice, Simon Narcisse Bozanga, call for the trial of Bokassa in absentia. Dacko then ordered the judgment of and death sentences for a number of other former accomplices of Bokassa.

This time such token acts gained Dacko little, if any, support in the Central African Republic. He undertook to place himself in a somewhat stronger position to negotiate with his only real source of power, the French government under Giscard d'Estaing. On September 22, 1980, Dacko was assured by the French president of sufficient French support to remain in power. In return, Dacko was to promise a new constitution and elections for president, and, later, a national assembly. This promise as well as his appointment of Jean-Pierre LeBouder, a thirty-six-year-old French-educated technocrat, as prime minister on November 12, 1980, and the calling of a "national seminar" to be held from December 8 through 14 to provide a forum for the exchange of ideas on the proposed new constitution, all bought Dacko time. These apparent steps toward a more liberal regime allowed the French government to assume a lower profile in the affairs of the Central African Republic.

Alarmed by the successful Libyan intervention into neighboring Chad at the end of 1980, Dacko and his French backers sought an accommodation with opposition forces in the CAR. On December 19, 1980, the case against the absent "emperor" opened in Bangui, and after a trial filled with irregularities, Bokassa was sentenced to death in absentia on November 23. A handful of Bokassa's closest associates who had been condemned to death in February and again in September were finally executed on January 21, 1981. Rumors that circulated in Bangui suggested that the six executed men knew too much about Bokassa's association with Dacko and the French president who was himself facing a strong election challenge.[8]

A constitution calling for a multiparty system of government with a strong emphasis on human rights was hurriedly ratified by a group of Dacko's supporters in December. The ordinance providing for the election was issued on January 5, 1981, and Dacko signed another ordinance on January 22 permitting the establishment and free operation of political parties. On February 1, 1981, a national referendum was held to approve the December constitution. This constitution provided for a president to be elected for a six-year term by universal suffrage and to serve a total of only two terms if reelected. It gave the president the right to appoint the prime minister and the other ministers. An elected national assembly was given fixed legal and budgetary authority and the right to censure the prime minister. The constitution also provided for a multiparty system, an independent judiciary, a constitutional council, and an advisory economic council.

Of the 859,447 voters, 97.43 percent cast their ballots in favor of the constitution. The stage was set for an open struggle among various members of the bureaucratic bourgeoisie to legitimize their control of the government of the Central African Republic. With only one or perhaps two exceptions they seemed to have been motivated essentially by the desire to hold a position that would guarantee them a share of the surplus to be extracted from the country. The needs and wishes to the majority of the people of the Central African Republic appear to have been completely left out. The populace counted only insofar as it constituted a political base that the bureaucratic bourgeoisie elite could exploit when it made a show of pursuing the people's interests. The only candidate with popular support was the forty-four-year-old Patassé who, though born at Paoua near the border with Chad in the northwestern part of the country, had become a favorite of young students and unemployed "street people" (*godabé* in Sango) of Bangui. This trained agronomist of Sara ethnic origins had been almost constantly in one ministry or another under Bokassa. Yet his unstructured and fluid mix of populist-left rhetoric had given his party, the MLPC, considerable notoriety. Patassé had suffered under Dacko. A French-supported grenade attack had destroyed his home in Bangui on October 30, 1979; he had endured numerous house arrests and imprisonment in the infamous Ngaragba prison. He was thus a natural focus for resistance to Dacko's oppression.

Henri Maidou was the alternative to Dacko perceived by many French and other outside observers to be the most intelligent and pro-French. At age forty-five, his major handicap from the viewpoint of most Central Africans was that he had been prime minister when Bokassa had massacred the schoolchildren in 1979. Maidou, like Dacko, had been a schoolteacher. He held a *license* (university degree) in geography, but his ambition far outstripped his popular support. His sudden dismissal by Dacko in 1980 had been met with an almost unanimous indifference on the part of Central Africans. His *Parti Progressife Républicain* was of little real consequence.

Though scarcely known by many of the younger generation of Central Africans, Maidou's brother-in-law, the fifty-three-year-old Abel Goumba, probably represented the most serious intellectual opposition to the Dacko regime. Goumba had been one of Boganda's closest and most loyal associates. Dacko had been successful, with French aid, in removing Goumba from power after Boganda's tragic death. Goumba, after having served more than two years in prison under Dacko, had gone into exile in mid-1962, completed his medical training, and had been serving with the World Health Organization as a physician in Rwanda and Benin (formerly Dahomey) until 1981 when he returned to Bangui. As the head of the FPO, which he had founded in 1976 from exile, Goumba drew his support chiefly from progressive elements in France plus a small circle of Bangui intellectuals. Yet as an honest, intelligent patriot who had spoken out against Bokassa from the first, who had never succumbed to French machination, and who was clearly Boganda's real heir, Goumba was an obvious embarrassment to Dacko.

Another candidate was the forty-five-year-old, Bangassou-born bureaucrat, François Pehoua. He had served briefly in 1971 as a minister in Bokassa's government but had spent most of his career with the *Banque des Etats de l'Afrique Centrale* (BEAC). His *Groupement Indépendent de Reflexion* (GIR) was less a party than a group of moderate government bureaucrats and technicians who opposed Dacko's growing personal usurpation of power. Pehoua was a respected associate of Robert Galley, the French banking adviser, and had been encouraged to enter the contest by backers in Paris who were not sure that Dacko would withstand the Patassé challenge.

A final candidate of lesser importance was the Mobaye-born magistrate, François Gueret. At age forty-five he had already served as minister of justice, labor, public functions, social affairs, administration reform, Central Africanization, and state finance in Dacko's first cabinet. Gueret had lived in exile during the Bokassa regime and was known for his lack of corruption. He had resigned from Dacko's government in 1980, protesting that Dacko was not vigorous in prosecuting certain "untouchable" accomplices of Bokassa. His *Mouvement pour la Démocratie et l'Indépendence* (MDI) was characterized by a virulent anti-Sovietism and manifested among its few young supporters an occasional pro-Chinese leftist bent.

Patassé had served in at least eleven different ministerial posts under Bokassa and had been Bokassa's penultimate prime minister. With 238,739 votes out of the total 744,680, Patassé was the major factor in limiting Dacko to a narrow 0.23 percent margin over the 50 percent necessary to avoid a runoff.[9]

Even with the advantages that the incumbent enjoyed such as the vehicles newly furnished by the French government for the Ministry of Health, which Dacko used for campaign purposes, overt election rigging, and other election irregularities, it was clear that Dacko was not the overwhelming choice of the Central African people. He was certainly not the choice of the more sophisticated population of Bangui that represented 20 percent of the nation's voters. In Bangui Dacko received only 37,500 votes against Patassé's 42,550. Two days of riots and demonstrations followed the announcement of election results in Bangui and Bossangoa, in the Markounda area near the Chad border that was Patassé's ethnic stronghold. Dacko took advantage of the situation to declare a state of emergency, send French troops into Bossangoa and Bangui, and move to appoint his supporters to as many key positions as possible in the new government.

Immediately after the new government was formed, Dacko called a congress of the UDC. He had his Prime Minister Simon Narcisse Bozanga, his Minister of Education Pierre Sammy Mack Foy, his Minister of Finance Barthélemy Kanda, and his Minister of Foreign Affairs Jean-Pierre Kombet voted to membership on the party's central committee. A UDC militia was established and several hundred of its members were armed to deal with opposition-controlled areas of Bangui. Four of the opposition leaders, Ange Patassé, Henri Maidou, Abel Goumba, and François Pehoua called on the Supreme Court to annul the elections on the grounds of vote rigging. With little hope of success they moved to create a *Conseil Politique Provisoire* (CPP) to support a single list of candidates for the legislative elections. Fearing the outcome, Dacko forbade the opposition the use of government-controlled radio and television on the grounds that supposedly they were encouraging "tribalism"; in early May 1981 Dacko announced that he was postponing legislative elections indefinitely until procedures could be reorganized and, significantly, the electoral maps could be redrawn and voter lists checked.

With the defeat of Giscard d'Estaing in the 1981 French election, Dacko's strong French support was gone. Without it Dacko turned to even more draconian measures to maintain his position. By the end of May, Dacko, seemingly confident in his preemptive measures, said that he believed that democracy in the Central

African Republic was at least ten years away. But President Dacko was not content to halt only the electoral process. On May 14, Dacko had set up a government union, the *Confédération Nationale des Travailleurs Centrafricains* (CNTC) with his mouthpiece, Richard Sandos, as its secretary-general. The country's only free union, the 15,000-strong *Union Générale des Travailleurs Centrafricains* (UGTCA), called a strike in the private sector for May 15 (despite strong criticism from Dacko's government) in sympathy with workers at a French-owned firm who, it was alleged, had been unjustly discharged, threatened, and even arrested. The strike had a good response, but when the UGTCA announced that it would call out the public-sector workers the next day, Dacko promptly ordered the union disbanded. The union's secretary-general was termed "armed and dangerous" by the Dacko government and was forced to flee. Dozens of other workers were also rounded up and detained while Dacko's government ignored queries by international unions. Dacko underlined his point in early June by introducing close censorship, with all outgoing reports to international agencies subject to scrutiny by Information Minister Alphonse Blagué, another Dacko loyalist.

As Dacko's drive to increase his power escalated, the opposition increased its activities as well. Faced with an increasingly illiberal regime, a tenuous united front drew together the losing candidates from the March presidential elections, and former Minister of Justice François Gueret, in the *Conseil Politique Provisoire* (CPP). The political differences among the various members of this group, though, made them far from effective. Among the five major contenders for power, Ange Patassé seemed to pose the most immediate threat to Dacko.

A final member of this loose coalition was Rodolphe Iddi Lala. Dr. Iddi Lala's *Mouvement Centrafricain de Libération Nationale* (MCLN) and its military wing the *Forces Armée's de Libération Militaire* appeared to be largely a paper creation. At forty-five he held a doctorate in sociology and had taught for a number of years in Brazzaville. Expelled from Goumba's FPO in July 1980 where he had been in charge of external relations, Iddi Lala was certainly one of the wild cards in the loose opposition coalition formed to oppose Dacko.

On July 14 a bomb exploded in Le Club, one of the most popular movie houses in Bangui, killing three people and wounding a dozen or so others. The MCLN claimed responsibility and maintained that this was the first of many terrorist actions, which would continue until the French troops left. Dacko ordered a state of siege and banned not only the MCLN but also the FPO and the MLPC, although leaders of the CPP groups had condemned the action. Opposition leaders were arrested, including Patassé, but not Goumba, who had fled to Paris saying that he feared for his life. From Paris the CPP issued a statement calling for Dacko's resignation. It also sent a letter to Dacko accusing him of fomenting ethnic hatred, preventing freedom of expression, and dismissing all civil servants who did not belong to the UDC. Allegations were also made that Dacko was setting up an Mbaka militia.[10] At the end of July Dacko did promote a number of army officers, including André Kolingba, a member of a riverine ethnic group, the Yakoma, which was closely related to Dacko's own Mbaka group. Major General Kolingba became a full general, and Dacko's dependence on the army became quite apparent.

Under the new presidency of François Mitterrand, the French were becoming increasingly embarrassed at propping up President Dacko, not only because of their wish to make a clean break with Giscard's African policy, but also because of the increasing documentation presented by the CPP of the steady erosion of human rights taking place in the Central African Republic. During August, aware that his position was becoming ever more precarious, Dacko lifted the ban on the MLPC and the FPO and then lifted the state of siege. The MCLN was still declared illegal. It was clear that without resort to force, Dacko's days were numbered. In a press conference on August 4 he had stated the truism that "when the army demands that the president step down it is a coup d'état."

KOLINGBA REGIME

Early in the morning of September 1, 1981, units under the command of Army Chief of Staff General André Kolingba rolled into position in Bangui and once again enacted a charade coup against an already defeated Dacko. At the end of July Kolingba had already suggested to Dacko that he resign. Although Dacko refused this suggestion, he did acquiesce to naming Kolingba's close associate, Lieutenant Colonel Christophe Grelombe, head of gendarmes. By discharging Commandant Sylvestre N'Dayen, the brother of the archbishop of Bangui, and without French troops to back him, Dacko placed himself completely at the mercy of Kolingba.

It was not surprising therefore that well before dawn on a Tuesday morning a month later General Kolingba asked for and received Dacko's resignation "in order to put an end to the political disorder." In an interview with *Agence France Presse* a few days later Kolingba said he had seized power because Dacko's government and the opposition parties grouped in the CPP had been behaving like two "punch-drunk" boxers. "Someone had to stop them," he said, "and in the public interest, I intervened."[11]

General André Kolingba took power with the de facto acceptance of the CPP and certainly with no overt opposition from the populace. It also appears that this former Central African ambassador to West Germany and Canada had at least the tacit approval of the Mitterrand government because none of the 1,200 to 1,500 French troops in the country offered any opposition to his assuming authority. Even Dacko's Praetorian Guard, his "green berets" composed of Mbaka troops specially trained by French paracommandos (quick strike paratroopers) and under the command of Colonel Mention, offered absolutely no resistance. On September 1, 1981, the army of the Central African Republic consisted of about 1,900 men with 7 generals and a dozen colonels.

The Kolingba seizure was not simply a barracks coup. Kolingba, unlike his predecessor Bokassa, was a graduate of French military schools in Brazzaville and Frejus and came to power with considerable support from the Central African bureaucratic bourgeoisie. Among these supporters the most prominent were Bernard-Christian Ayandho, a former prime minister under Dacko; Jean-Marie Songomali, upper-level bureaucrat in the *Agence de Coopération Culturelle et Technique* (ACCT); and Michel Gallin-Douthe, a man in his sixties who had been an administrator in the French Ministry of the Interior (he held dual nationality) and who had come out of retirement to help the new government.

These key members of Kolingba's Yakoma ethnic group represented a major power shift from Dacko's "presidential clique" that had been increasingly composed of his own kinsmen and family members. Yet the larger "ruling brotherhood" of selected members of other ethnic groups and their clients and the few technocratically competent members of the bureaucratic bourgeoisie changed little. From the beginning Commandant Jean Allan, interior secretary of state, was Ange Patassé's friend and General Sylvestre Yangongo, minister of labor, was a brother of one of Abel Goumba's closest associates. Furthermore, although a number of the new government officials were quite competent, most lacked experience and many were simply incompetent. Finally, it should not be forgotten that Kolingba's decision to take over came as a result of the huge welcoming demonstration for Ange Patassé staged by his supporters at the Bangui-M'Poko airport on August 31. Kolingba took office determined to eliminate such political threats to national unity.

As president of the twenty-three-member *Comité Militaire de Redressement National* (CMRN) that replaced Dacko's government on September 1, 1981, Kolingba affirmed that the army would not establish a military dictatorship. His immediately announced aim was to get the economy back on its feet so that every Central African could have a decent standard of living. This, of course, necessitated external aid, and Kolingba called on all African countries to lend "fraternal" support and upon the French to maintain and even increase their economic support. One-third of the Central African government's budget in 1981 was supplied by external aid. "We must be given time to feed the population before we can think of democracy" was Kolingba's reply to questions from Mitterrand's government about a free election. "In six months, maybe in a year, I don't know" was his reply in the first week of power. "But in any case, it won't be immediately."

Kolingba's first major step toward economic recovery was the promise of a reduction in and reorganization of the bloated civil and diplomatic services. In late September he even stated that he would reduce the military by a thousand before the end of 1981. Kolingba further promised tht corruption and misappropriation of government funds would be severely punished. Kolingba began by agreeing to carry out the budget suggestions that Dacko had been forced to accept from France and the International Monetary Fund (IMF). With a budget deficit of 11 billion CFA francs projected for 1981 and 14 billion for 1982, there was little else he could do. Suspending all union and political activities, freezing all government salaries for 1982, and promising strong support for the private sector, Kolingba approached the first months in office as if he were executing a military campaign. Consulting to a limited extent with members of the CMRN, he personally directed the country by means of the existing civil service and state apparatus. Kolingba made few promises but rather warned of the years of hard work and austerity, necessary to redress past errors.

The political honeymoon period for General Kolingba's military government was even more short lived than that afforded Dacko in his second term. By January 1982 rumors of plots and counterplots became the order of the day as free and open political activities were suppressed. By March 3, 1982, events had already come to a head. At 11:00 P.M. General Simon Bozize, then minister of information, broadcast a radio message. This former favorite of Bokassa accused General Kolingba of treason and announced that he was taking power. As he had been in the airport security the night Bokassa was overthrown, Bozize had some experience with coups d'état. About one-half hour later Adjoint Army Chief of Staff Colonel François Diallo refuted Bozize's statement, and about midnight General Kolingba himself went on the air and reminded listeners why he and the CMRN had taken power. The situation in most of Bangui remained calm, but at Kilometre Cinq[12] and elsewhere in the shantytowns of the capital, rioting and looting rapidly became the rule. Ange Patassé, who had staged another of his grand returns to Central Africa from France only five days earlier, immediately declared from his home compound that he was the president of the Central African Republic by popular acclaim and that elections ought to be called immediately.[13]

Claiming a strong possibility that Patassé had Libyan or even Soviet support, Kolingba reacted swiftly. Attacking the MLPC and its president as a major threat to the nation's internal security, Kolingba ordered Patassé and other party members arrested early on the morning of March 4. Patassé remained in hiding until March 7 when he and some of his supporters sought political asylum at the French embassy. Mitterrand's government exhibited some reluctance to grant Patassé asylum, but when Kolingba's government issued an ultimatum to the French to deliver him,

French pride caused them to stiffen their position and recognize his "right of asylum." Patassé had, however, overestimated his French support.

The immediate result of Patassé's aborted coup was Kolingba's turn toward a hard-line approach to opponents. In July 1982 French Minister for Cooperation and Development Jean-Pierre Cot bade a special welcome to Goumba, which upset Kolingba and led to speculation that France was unhappy about the conduct of Kolingba's military government, particularly the evident lack of progress toward a return to constitutional rule. Then in August 1982 Kolingba had Abel Goumba arrested, maintaining that Goumba and the FPO were organizing a movement to destabilize the government of the Republic. At a trial filled with irregularities on April 22, 1983, Goumba, whom Kolingba had appointed rector of the University of Bangui, and Patrice Endjimougou, the secretary-general of the FPO, were sentenced to five years imprisonment. They were both also fined two million CFA francs. Their main crime seems to have been corresponding with the French Socialist party. Given Kolingba's reliance on French government subsidies, a support committee headed by Pierre Kalck succeeded in having Goumba freed from Ngaragba prison within four months.

The information spread in September 1983 that the FPO, the MLPC, and the MCLN had joined together on August 5 to create a new party, the *Parti Révolutionaire Centrafricain* (PRC), with the goal of overturning the Kolingba government, was denied by the leaders of both the MLPC and the FPO. The supposed clandestine meeting at Moyenne-Sido in northern Central African Republic of the leaders of the three main opposition groups would seem to have been fabricated by members of Kolingba's government to discredit the MLPC and the FPO in the eyes of the French by associating these parties with the Libyan-connected MCLN. In mid-September 1983 the MLPC did hold an extraordinary congress in Central Africa and removed the mercurial Ange Patassé, in exile in Togo, from office. In his place a new group of far more pragmatic leaders including Francis-Albert Ouakanga, Jacques Boniba, and Raphael Nambele took control. Both these leaders and the FPO under Goumba made it clear that they wished to disassociate themselves from extralegal means of redressing the nation's difficulties.

In like manner both parties rejected the opéra bouffe attempt by ex-Emperor Bokassa to return to Bangui on November 27, 1983. His plan to fly into Bangui from his Ivory Coast exile in the company of lawyers, bodyguards, and his French public relations expert, Roger Delpey, was thwarted by the French intelligence services. The venture, which was allegedly financed by four large international companies in return for promises of uranium, diamond, and ivory concessions, never got off the ground. Tipped off by the French, officials in the Ivory Coast grounded the expedition's plane upon its arrival in Abidjan from Paris. Expelled from the Ivory Coast, Bokassa flew to Paris in December 1983 where he was granted permission to stay temporarily by French foreign minister, Claude Cheysson. Bokassa, as a former member of the French armed forces and owner of extensive properties in France, claimed French nationality and asserted that he would be allowed to stay indefinitely.

From rather hopeful beginnings, Kolingba's government rapidly moved once again toward the single ethnic group and personalized rule that characterizes most postindependence African dictatorships. As early as October 3, 1982, Kolingba had pushed back until 1985 any possibility of elections or a return to civilian rule. Corruption and favoritism again became the order of the day. Civil liberties and legal recourse were once again limited and arbitrary rule once more became the norm. The old guard of French settlers and companies again regained a stronghold on the country's economy while Kolingba and his close ethnic supporters returned to the precolonial tradition of "big men" systems of the forest zone, which had evolved during the long years of the slave trade.[14] Reshuffling ministers at will, Kolingba rules as president of the CMRN, prime minister, minister of defense and veterans, and chief of staff of the army over a handpicked group of military officers with eight civilian "high commissioners."

Unfortunately, Kolingba's initial attempts to establish economic prosperity were not very successful. The country's continuing debt-service problems, aggravated by a rate of exchange unfavorable to the Central African Repubic of the dollar against the CFA franc, the failure to curb government spending and in particular to rein in civil service costs caused the IMF to suspend credit payments after the first $4.5 million were drawn in August 1983. Faced with a revenue shortfall of 8 billion CFA francs for 1983, General Sylvestre Bangui, Kolingba's economic and finance minister, flew to Washington in September where he was forced to agree on new harsher budget guidelines and ceilings on domestic credit.

Kolingba's response was not calculated to restore the country's already very slim international creditworthiness. On January 17, 1984, the Central African Republic's military committee rejected the austerity budget drawn up by the IMF and published a 1984 budget projecting a 22 percent increase in expenditure and an increased deficit of nearly 10 billion CFA francs for 1984. General Bangui was dismissed six days later for failing to defend the new budget. Neither additional revenue nor greatly increased subsidies from France have been forthcoming. The present government of the Central African Republic faces imminent bankruptcy, and it is unlikely that the 5.5 billion CFA franc interest-free loan that General Kolingba negotiated in Beijing during a presidential visit of July 4–8, 1983, will be repeated.

In spite of some initial reluctance on the part of President Mitterrand and his Socialist government, the Central African Republic's relations with France had virtually returned to their time-honored patterns by the end of Kolingba's first year in power. France continues to pay more than 5 billion CFA francs as budgetary support and to supply some 400 technical assistants in addition to the 1,200–1,500-strong garrison of French troops through 1985. In addition, France indirectly supports more than 4,000 other French nationals in residence by maintaining a very visible presence in the country.

NOTES

1. Much of the material in this section is based upon Pierre Kalck, *Histoire de la République Centrafricaine* (Paris: Editions Berger-Levrault, 1974), 302–314.

2. This section also draws upon Kalck, *Histoire de la République Centrafricaine*, 314–332, for much detail and Jacques Serre, "Six ans de gouvernement Dacko (1960–1966), *Revue française d'études politiques Africaines* 117 (Sept. 1975), 73–104.

3. Dacko eventually freed Goumba and allowed him to leave the country to complete his medical training after more than two years in jail.

4. Kalck, *Histoire de la République Centrafricaine,* p. 331.

5. A complete history of the Bokassa era remains to be written. This outline is drawn from newspaper sources and personal interviews with firsthand observers.

6. The United States offered the new regime fifty-seven Peace Corps volunteers on February 8, 1966.

7. A word in Sango, the Central African lingua franca, with three meanings: the place of lineage origins, the village, and the section of town where one resides. Though *akodro* would be the correct plural of the singular *kodro,* the Anglicization *kodros* is used here for convenience.

8. See, for example, *Le Matin* (Sept. 25, 1980), 3; Zilegue, "Bilan? Désastreux," *Afrique Asie* 224 (Oct. 13, 1980), 42–44 and *West Africa* (Mar. 2, 1981).

9. Election information is based upon results reported by the Central African Supreme Court four days after the election. See "La ré-élection au premier tour de président Dacko," *Afrique Contemporaine* 115 (May-June 1981), 24–25.

10. *African Contemporary Record,* 1980, p. B409.

11. "Someone had to stop them," *Africa News* 17:10 (Sept. 7, 1981), 7–8.

12. In Bangui, the various areas are frequently identified by the distance in kilometers from the center of town.

13. Jean-Claude Pomonti, "Le général Kolingba a dejoué une tentative de coup d'état des partisans de M. Patassé," *Le Monde* (Mar. 5, 1982), 7.

14. See Thomas E. O'Toole, "Jean-Bedel Bokassa: Neo-Napoleon or Traditional African Ruler?" in *The Cult of Power: Dictators in the Twentieth Century,* ed. Joseph Held (New York: Columbia University Press, 1983), 95–106.

4

Society and Change

The Central African government, following the wise course charted by Boganda, pronounced at independence that ethnic distinctions should play no role in the political and social life of the country. The wisdom of this political decision has been largely borne out by contemporary research that recognizes that ethnic groups are not discrete entities. Rather, ethnic groups are open, and their membership and identity shift constantly. This is especially true in the Central African Republic where ethnic groups have come together, changed, and disappeared frequently throughout the past.[1]

In considering the question of ethnicity in the present-day CAR one needs to remember that ethnicity is not simply a classification created by external analysis. Ethnicity also exists from the viewpoints of people who are thus classified. These two aspects are often difficult to keep analytically distinct. The first is a relatively clean, objective social science consideration regarding the ethnographic pigeonholing of Central African peoples by ascribing to them specific and relatively fixed customs, behaviors, and values according to more or less objectively arrived at archetypes. The second aspect is a far more difficult and complex question involving individual self-perceptions, which do not always correspond to externally established categories. Many ethnic groups in the Central African Republic, whatever their origins, had become culturally quite analogous by the late nineteenth century. Yet today most Central Africans still live within disrupted but nevertheless still persisting communitarian, lineage-based economic and political communities. These communities can be mobilized and organized for collective action by the bureaucratic bourgeoisie for its own ends by means of "ethnicization" of relative or absolute deprivation and real or supposed threats to the communities. Hence it is valuable to de-emphasize the ethnic preoccupations that caused most French administrators to attempt to separate Central Africans into fixed ethnic groups. At the same time one should remain quite aware of the existence of more subtle ethnic cleavages operating within ethnologically homogeneous populations.

HISTORICAL ETHNICITY

In 1952 the colonial administration fixed the number of ethnic groups in the Central African territory at eight; this grouping was based loosely on cultural characteristics. The eight included: Gbaya-Manja (Mandja or Manza), Banda, Ubangians, Sara, Zande, Nzakara, Muslims, and Cameroonians. The Muslims included both the floating populations of Muslim traders found throughout much of the country and the former subjects of the sultanate of Dar al-Kuti. The latter were frequently people of Banda origin who had accepted Islam generations earlier.

"Muslim," clearly, is not an ethnic identity. It was simply a term used by Europeans and others in the Central African Republic to group together Central Africans who had been influenced by Islam. In much the same manner the term *Ubangian* was used by the French administration to group together the varied and mixed river-trading peoples who lived in the Ubangi Valley between the Kemo and Mbomu rivers. These populations included Mbaka, Yakoma, Bantu-speaking groups in the Haute-Sangha, and others. Most of the bureaucratic bourgeoisie that has manipulated Central African politics since World War II have come from these riverine groups. Finally, the term "Cameroonian" simply referred to the refugee populations in the mountain communities of the northwest, who had fled the Adamawa Plateau at the time of the Fulbé invasions.

With the exception of the small Muslim minority (scarcely more than 20,000) and an undetermined but large and growing number of people with little if any religious affiliation, the vast majority of Central Africans are about equally divided between putative adherents of Christianity and participants in traditional African religions. European schooling and religious instruction,

Central Africans are ethnically diverse. Photo courtesy of Barry Hewlett.

along with the impact of urban lifestyles and the decline of lineage-based authority, have eroded traditional African values. Most young urban Central Africans do not receive the training in ethics and social behavior that they would have been exposed to in village and lineage-based societies. Basically left to fend for themselves, their socialization process offers little training in the values that make for socially constructive behavior. Their largely superficial exposure to Christianity does not represent a viable alternative. In terms of day-to-day behavior, especially among the youth in Bangui and in the larger administrative centers, Christianity appears to have far less impact than traditional patterns once had in rural areas. Many maintain that this accounts for the general instability of present-day Central African society.[2]

Today about one-half of the population of Central Africa is nominally Christian. About one-half of these are Roman Catholic and the other half is divided among a number of Protestant groups. The Roman Catholics are still very much under the tutelage of various European missionary groups, and the Protestants are divided among various foreign-directed denominations for the most part. There are only a dozen or so Central African priests and about the same number of African religious sisters and brothers. There are some ministerial students but few, if any, active ordained Central African Protestant ministers. There are also a number of lay Protestant religion teachers. Given the high rates of venereal disease, alcoholism, and theft in the Central African Republic, it would seem that the ethics of Christianity, at present, have little impact on the value systems of the majority of Central African people.

Although Central African ethnic groups have always been fluidly ethnic, and identity persists as a factor in present-day Central African political life, one needs some understanding of the evolution of the many indigenous societies in order to make sense of the complexities of precolonial history in the area. Given the lack of written sources and the generally shallow time depth for oral traditions in the Central African Republic, historians have turned to linguists for help in reconstructing the ethnohistory of the country. Based on linguistic evidence, it is clear that the Republic has been a crossroads for human migration for millennia. Living in the Central African Republic today are groups that speak (as their first language) a language from three of the four major African language phyla developed by the linguist J. H. Greenberg.[3]

Only one of Greenberg's phyla does not have a language presently spoken in the Central African Republic—the Khoisan phylum that includes the click languages spoken by populations of Namibia, Botswana, and the Republic of South Africa. A number of groups speak languages belonging to Greenberg's broad Afro-Asiatic phylum, and among these are many groups speaking Arabic. Scattered throughout the country are several different populations speaking various Chadic languages of this phylum, including the

Traditional religious initiations and Christianity coexist in the CAR. Photos courtesy of Thomas O'Toole and Barry Hewlett, respectively.

Hausa lingua franca. The Nilo-Saharan phylum is not notably present as a Chari-Nile language spoken by Sara populations, but other Nilo-Saharan language families exist among populations coming from or influenced by peoples from Sudan.

The Niger-Kordofanian phylum, especially the Niger-Congo cluster, is the most completely represented grouping. A form of Fulfuldé, an example of the West Atlantic language family belonging to this cluster, is spoken by the nomadic Bororo populations of the country, while the Adamawa-Ubangian subdivision of the phylum has a number of languages represented, including Gbaya, Zande, and Sango. This latter language, originating among the riverine canoeing populations of the Ubangi River, had gradually become the lingua franca of trade along most of the tributaries of the river by the end of the nineteenth century. With French military occupation, Sango spread throughout the Ubangi-Shari territory, even spilling over into Chad and the Moyen-Congo.

In the 1920s Reverend William Haas of the Mid-Africa Mission (Baptist Mid-Missions) began work with a group of missionaries of a Mid-Africa Mission Language Committee to develop a written form of Sango. The committee worked with Central Africans to establish a standardized grammar and pronunciation. Ultimately they produced the first major written work in Sango, a New Testament, which fixed a near-French orthography for this language.[4] Since independence Sango, along with French, has been the official language of the Central African Republic.

French, an Indo-European language, remains an important language for the Western-educated minority in the Central African Republic and is the language of instruction at the secondary and university levels. French is necessary for external communication and commerce and could scarcely be replaced by any other language. Occasional attempts to make Sango the only official language have never seriously challenged the de facto official status of French.

For the most part it is useful to employ a less complicated system to group present-day Central Africans than that used by the ethnohistorians. It is possible to use two general groupings for almost all indigenous Central Africans.[5] The first group, the speakers of Central Sudanic languages—the western subdivision of which includes the major languages of northern and eastern

Today's river people have a wide variety of ethnic origins. Photo courtesy of Barry Hewlett.

Central African Republic, probably spread into the area from southwestern Sudan more than 1,000 years ago. The populations speaking these languages, such as the Sara and Kara, were by the year 1400 millet and sorghum cultivators. Their initial expansion south and west into the area may well have taken place only as the development of new strains of millet and sorghum allowed expansion into these more humid areas. Herding cattle, goats, and possibly sheep, they originally lived in small, basically egalitarian villages widely scattered throughout the northern fringes of what is now the wooded savanna of the Central African Republic.

The second language branch can be labeled Ubangian. It is a branch of the larger Adamawa-Ubangian group that probably spread through the southern savanna of the Central African Republic from the Adamawa Massif before A.D. 1000. People speaking Ubangian languages, such as Banda, Manja, and Gbaya, predominated throughout most of the better watered southern half of the country between the dry savanna and the forest. They used mainly West African agricultural techniques. These groups were in the region before the Central Sudanic speakers penetrated very deeply into the area. At present in the Republic about 400,000 persons would probably identify themselves as Banda. The second most numerous savanna population, about 350,000 people, is the Gbaya. Today most Gbaya live in the northeast of the country, although a small number of closely related Manja are on the south bank of the Ubangi River in the forest zone. About 80,000 Mbum, whose ancestors once formed an Adamawa Plateau federation, are also found in the Central African Republic. The vast majority of this population remained in Cameroon, and those groups found in the CAR today persist as very poor refugee populations.

In the southwestern forest areas of the Central African Republic some of the Ubangi-speaking populations, including the Banziri, the Sango, the Yakoma, and, especially the Mbaka, were influenced by the Atlantic slave-trading economy even before the nineteenth century and played an important intermediary role between the Bantu-speaking populations to the south and west and the Arab-influenced populations to the east. The location of the Ubangi speakers also placed them in first contact with the European colonizers and consequently gave them the most immediate access to European education. Under the colonial administration the more "Europeanized" members of these groups developed into a petit bourgeois quasi class that relied entirely on the colonial capitalist system for its salaries and wages—indeed for its very survival. In time, elements of this class evolved into the indigenous bureaucratic bourgeoisie that has dominated the political life of the Central African Republic since the late 1950s. The forest populations also include the Aka ("Pygmies"), who number about 16,000 today. This "exotic" minority of nomadic hunters and gatherers has little future as an identifiable group because the forest is being cut down and village populations are placing pressure on the Aka's fragile symbiotic relationship with the forest.

Three other groups that do not fit well into the above categories are important enough for special mention. The Azande, descendants of the great kingdoms of the nineteenth century, today number less that 20,000. The Fulbé Bororos (perhaps 15,000) hold a virtual monopoly on cattle herding and can be found throughout the western part of the CAR. Small groups of Islamized traders, popularly termed Hausas, have been established in or near the major towns in the western and central part of the country since early in the colonial era. These Hausas[6] constitute more than 75 percent of the small traders in the country although they number far fewer than 10,000.

THE DEMOGRAPHIC TIMEBOMB

The colonial administration of Ubangi-Shari took a number of population surveys, but none of them was very accurate. Central African villages inevitably associate a census with the head tax, the compulsory cultivation of cotton, or some other form of taxation and avoid enumeration whenever possible. Given the inadequacy of survey techniques and the general resistance to a census, a substantial minority of Central Africans continue to be able to evade any attempt to count them.

The first population count after independence was based on French administration figures, and on December 31, 1962, the government fixed the population of the Central African Republic at 1,279,642 persons. (It should be noted that only a small proportion of either deaths or births are registered and birth certificates are usually given out for a fee.) The 1962 census represented a gain of about 200,000 over the 1952 tally published by the French. In 1965, Dacko called for a more exhaustive census that produced a total population of 2,088,000—almost exactly 1 million more than in 1952. On the whole, these numbers were not considered valid by most informed observers.

In 1979 the government accepted the results of the 1975 sample census that estimated a total population of 2,057,000. This estimate was more accurate than a previous figure of over 3 million that the Bokassa government had promulgated, and it corresponded more closely to the mid-1982 estimates of 2 million suggested by informed experts.[7]

It is estimated that the annual rate of population increase is about 2.3 percent. Until very recently a high death rate, especially for children, compensated for the extraordinarily high birthrate (5 percent). Deaths for children under one year of age currently reach 190 per 1000. Obviously, if better prenatal and postnatal care and better health practices in general were to lower this figure, a veritable population bomb would be set to explode in the Central African Republic. Young people under fifteen constitute at least 40 percent of the population while people over sixty are scarcely more than 6.5 percent of the population.[8]

The explosive demand for relevant social services, food, clothing, education, housing, health services, and job opportunities that this youthful population represents can not be met by the present growth potential of the economy. Runaway urbanization and the current rates of unemployment already threaten the social and political stability of the country. Clearly some radical policy changes are called for if the Central African Republic is to avoid a population crisis.

At present the population of the Republic is overwhelmingly rural. Less than 30 percent of the population lives in the capital, Bangui, and the small towns that have grown around former colonial administrative posts. Throughout the country there are more than 6,000 villages with fewer than 100 people; a majority of these vilages are found toward the Ubangi in the southwest and also in the northwest. Three secondary towns with 35,000–93,000 inhabitants (Berbérati, 93,000; Bouar, 51,000; and Bossangoa, 35,0000 scarcely count as urban centers because most of their

Place Boganda with the Ubangi River in the background. Photo courtesy of Thomas O'Toole.

populations earn at least some of their livelihood from rural pursuits—hunting, gathering, and farming. Bangui is the only real urban area. In 1934 the population of Bangui was only about 19,000, but by 1966 the city had grown to 152,000, and in 1985 there were more than 350,000 people living in this capital city.

With a relatively sparsely populated hinterland and only one real urban center, the whole of the landlocked Central African Republic focuses on Bangui for access to the larger world. Like most other African cities, after World War II Bangui experienced accelerated growth that became even more rapid after independence. The reasons for this rapid growth are hardly unique to Bangui. People flocked to the city seeking a better life. They came for better health care and schools and to find salaried employment, not necessarily because they wanted to escape rural life. Bangui is the only city in the CAR with a reasonably certain supply of electricity, medicine, or gasoline. It has a few hard-surfaced streets and the only fully staffed hospital in the country. Almost all government civil servants live in Bangui. Those officials who are posted to the provinces consider themselves exiles and spend far too much time in the capital city away from their assignments.

What was once an European settler town situated along the river and astride the rapids is now a bustling city centered around the Place de la République and along Avenue Boganda. From earliest colonial times through its three principal urban-renewal plans in 1946, 1967, and 1971, Bangui has remained a highly segregated city. Expatriates and the high-level Central African bureaucratic bourgeoisie live in the center of the city. Here also are the government palace, the ministries, the army headquarters, the embassies, the European commercial areas, and the residences of many of the wealthy—both foreign and Central African. To the west and north of this well-established and carefully constructed area are a number of other planned zones. Planned sections along the Avenue de France and Avenue Boganda that predate independence have such amenities as water and electricity. In these areas the houses are constructed of blocks and cement, sit on clearly defined rectangular lots, and are inhabited by relatively affluent civil servants and middle-income foreigners. Neither these older areas on the semiperiphery of the city nor newer housing areas to the north or east along the river are available to most Central Africans.

Away from the planned center and its semiperiphery, the city is composed of spontaneously created African *kodros.*[9] The most conspicuous of these *kodros* is Kilometre Cinq and its Mamadou-Mbaïka market covering 14,650 square meters and including many stories owned by Lebanese, Portuguese, and "Hausa" merchants. With its dusk-to-dawn bars and dance halls, this section of the city is virtually off-limits to non-*kodro* dwellers but is the center of urban life for many Central Africans. The city's largest and most important mosque is located in this hub of African-controlled commerce. MESAN, the political party that led the drive to independence in 1960, was established here in 1949. The founding father of independence for Central Africa, Barthélemy Boganda, chose Kilometre Cinq for his headquarters because, by its very existence, it represented an alternative to the colonial center of the city.

A single ethnic group often inhabits specific sections of the newer peripheral areas of the city. In these *kodros* one is struck by the strong resemblance to the rural lineage villages found throughout much of the Central African Republic. Often a *kodro,* like its rural counterpart, is named after its founder, who has immigrated from a rural area, and later residents give primary allegiance to descendants of this lineage leader. Municipal authorities also recognize these neighborhood leaders. A number of

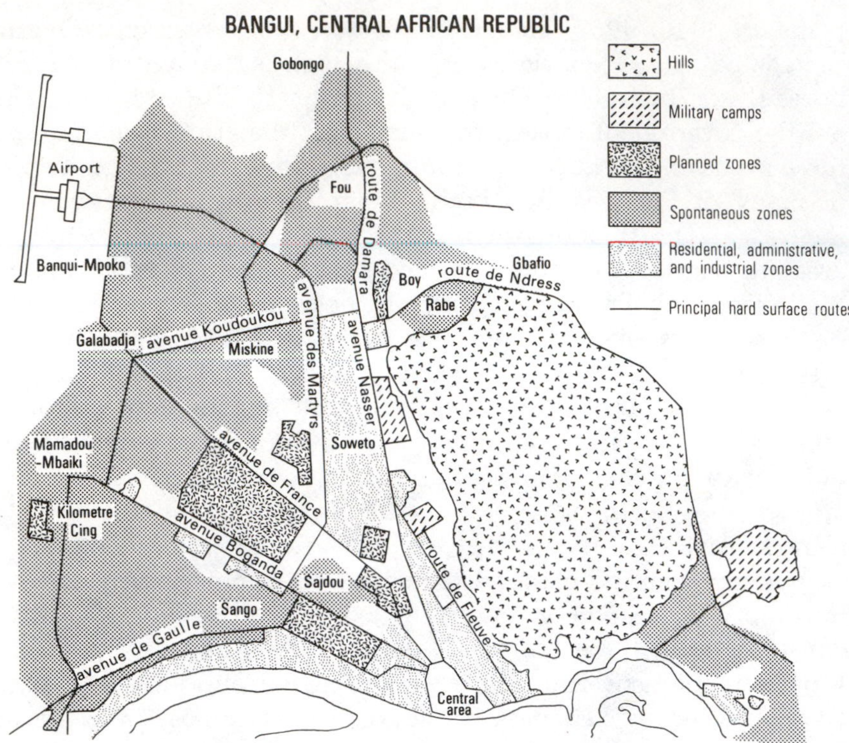

City of Bangui. Map courtesy of University of Minnesota Cartography Department.

such *kodros,* usually fewer than ten, are joined together to form larger communities such as Boy-Rabe, Miskine, or Sango. These groups are under the nominal direction of a *chef de groupe.* In theory these communities, which usually have their own school, market, and dispensary, are further united within one of the four arrondissements making up Bangui. This latter level of organization exists principally on paper for police purposes.

Within any given *kodro* a stranger can seldom distinguish regular patterns. Streets are rarely traced out in a fixed design because most travel and transport is by foot. With no boundary walls it is difficult for the uninitiated to avoid intruding on carefully defined living spaces that would be known and respected by the neighborhood's inhabitants. In the *kodro* the size of the houses, furnishings, and number of improvements like wells, cooking sheds, and bathing enclosures vary greatly from one owner to the next, an aspect of economic inequality that is less common in the more isolated rural areas. Houses are generally built of unbaked mud-brick by the owner with the help of relatives and friends. Most houses are rectangular in shape with thatched roofs of two or four slopes. Houses with metal or tile roofs are rare, and those with cement, plastered, or baked-brick walls are practically non-existent. Despite the differences in physical appearance between the *kodro* and rural villages, the persistence of the extended family, the feeling of solidarity among members of a similar age group from a particular geographical area, and the continued allegiance to the clan and the clan head make the social organization and the routines of daily life in the *kodro* fundamentally those of a rural village.

Major problems exist in these rural villages on the urban periphery. By and large the sanitary conditions are deplorable. With no sewer lines, open drainage presents real health problems. Most people draw their drinking water from hand-dug wells that lack proper curbing, so that diarrheal diseases and more serious water-borne illnesses are constant reality. Poor drainage, especially during the rainy season, crates mosquito-breeding areas that, in turn, cause malaria to persist as an endemic problem.

Two other problems appear to be approaching the crisis point in Bangui: lack of employment opportunities with the subsequent belief that self-improvement is impossible and lack of adequate food and fuel supplies. With a very small industrial and artisanal base, wage employment in Bangui is largely in the public sector or in the unskilled service sector. The public sector added more than 15,000 new positions in 1970 in a vain attempt to reduce the spiraling numbers of unemployed. Consequently the national budget was strained beyond its capacity to meet the monthly payroll. Government financing for any really productive and employment-generating projects thus becomes totally unavailable. The present regime continues, rather half-heartedly, to scale down this overinflated public sector.

The only sector of the economy that shows any vigor is trade. Both wholesale and retail trade in necessities like cloth, soap, and shoes, as well as the trade in luxury goods like motorbicycles and radios, is almost exclusively controlled by French, Portuguese, a variety of Southwest Asians, and Arab-speaking northerners (so-called Hausas). This is true both in the center of town and in the vigorous Kilometre Cinq emporiums and wooden kiosks. In contrast, the major open-air markets in town that specialize in the sale of foodstuffs are largely in the hands of local women.

Women's household and horticultural chores in the city are similar to those practiced in the home villages, but most *kodro* men find their urban employment differs greatly from their former village activities of hunting and millet farming. Even the forced cultivation of cotton, first under the colonial and then under the national regime, had little in common with the few salaried positions or the casual labor these men find. Working when they can as day laborers, mechanics' assistants, gardeners, domestic servants, and night watchmen, few men hold steady jobs and most have to piece together more than one means of livelihood. Most *kodro* men cultivate some food crops and put their children to work in gardening or in some cottage industry. Mud-brick making, sewing, bicycle repair, woodworking, and similar activities are all part of the ongoing lives of *kodro* households.

Although few formal surveys have been conducted among *kodro* populations, it is apparent that unemployed males, as a group, especially those under thirty, are less well adjusted to urban life than women or those few men who have found more or less steady employment. Among secondary and university students in Bangui a persistent sense of crisis is evident. They are very much aware of a generation gap and maintain that they have great difficulty making themselves understood by the older generation. Many express a strong desire to leave the Central African Republic for Cameroon, Congo, or, most often, France. Young *kodro* dwellers who are not in school seem to have much the same view. They tend, however, to be even more pessimistic. When questioned on what they thought would constitute progress for their areas of the city, they stated that more electrified homes, pharmacies, dispensaries, hard-surfaced roads, public water taps, better bus service, and access to schools would be crucial. Yet few see any way to play a role in bringing this improvement about and most, realistically, feel that the government is unlikely to do much to better their lives. *Kodro* youth even more than students tend to feel they are beaten before they start.[10]

Transport of plantains for selling by women. Photo courtesy of Daniel Gregory.

The second problem approaching a crisis point in the *kodro* is the increasing difficulty in supplying the daily food and fuel needs of the majority of the city's inhabitants. Manioc, the staple food, and cooking wood are trucked to Bangui from increasing distances at rapidly rising costs. Those Bangui residents who attempt to grow their own manioc find this more and more difficult. With some fields located ten or more kilometers from peoples' homes, self-sufficiency in the staple food becomes almost impossible. Small gardens of other food crops throughout the city and on its periphery, often tended by women, represent the slim margin of survival for a majority of people. Although most crops are consumed within the producer's household, rather than marketed, these garden products constitute a major part of the food supply for urban dwellers. In the late 1970s a movement back to the village in the countryside became increasingly noticeable, but it is not likely that this movement will ever achieve sufficient magnitude to solve Bangui's problems.

The present situation in Bangui appears quite unstable to most observers. And the city's future, like the future of many urban areas in black Africa, seems bleak. As elsewhere on the continent, cities are growing, military coups are commonplace, the price of imported goods is increasing, and many undesirable social changes are taking place. Large numbers of disaffected and unemployed urban people, especially the young, are turning to alcohol, cannabis, and other psychotropic drugs. Perhaps as many as 50 percent of the women between sixteen and twenty-one are unmarried, yet have one or more children with little or no paternal support. The surface disorder and squalor of the *kodros* lead the outsider to expect the worst: Riots, mass revolts, plague, and conflagrations appear to be just around the corner.[11]

A rural exodus to urban areas, especially Bangui, continues, leaving behind fewer cultivators. With little incentive to produce and few means to do so in any case, the average Central African cultivator can barely feed himself and his family, let alone produce a surplus to feed the essentially parasite urban populations. The overall level of nutrition in the Central African Republic, dangerously inadequate for more than a century, has reached a critical stage. Many people exhibit symptoms of marasmus, kwashiorkor, xerophthalmia, anemia, and endemic goiter. An inadequate food supply has been compounded in recent years by drought and continued erosion and soil degradation especially in the forest area, and the result is a crisis situation.[12]

Tuberculosis, venereal diseases of all types, yaws, bilharzia, leprosy, and other tropical diseases are endemic in the general population. Dysenteries (amoebic, bacillary, and other parasitic types), skin infections and rashes, malaria, and hepatitis are commonplace. Respiratory ailments are aggravated by seasonal dust and smoke pollution from cooking fires in Bangui and elsewhere in the country.

Overall health conditions of the majority of Central Africans are probably worse today than they were in precolonial times. Modern medical care is not available to most and, for all practical purposes, traditional curing practices have virtually disappeared. Village medical practice today consists of a few efficacious herbal remedies and many worthless or even harmful practices. Most people go without medical care unless they have access to the hospitals and dispensaries of the various Christian missions. In a few of the larger towns inadequate medical care is available at government-run hospitals and dispensaries. In Bangui there is one large government hospital, staffed primarily by French and French-trained staff. At present this hospital has specialists in ophthalmology, orthopedics, obstetrics and gynecology, general surgery, dermatology, and pediatrics. Even this hospital is not noted for its sanitation, and those who can afford it use private doctors and a small, thirteen-bed private clinic with limited facilities. Several medical laboratories operate in Bangui, and local pharmacies stock good supplies of medicine, principally from France. Dental care and routine optical service exists only in Bangui.

WOMEN AND SOCIAL CHANGE

The actual living situation of the majority of Central African women has not been systematically studied. Neither the impact of the French colonial regime nor the onset of independence has seriously altered the rural patterns of life that have been evolving for centuries. Most Central African women continue to play a crucial role in food gathering, production, conservation, distribution, and preparation. Hunting and fishing, male occupations, remain important for subsistence for many Central Africans, and the production of such commercial crops as coffee and cotton tends to be chiefly a male activity. It may safely be said, though, that women are the principal producers of food for household consumption. When one considers that they are also simultaneously involved in virtually all of the child-care responsibilities and much cottage industry, it becomes clear that underemployment and unemployment throughout Central Africa is almost exclusively a male phenomenon.

Although data on the precolonial era are fragmentary, it appears that, in most ethnic communities, women's rights were clearly defined and parallel to men's. Women apparently enjoyed a great deal of sexual freedom prior to and even during marriage, could divorce their husbands, could own personal possessions, and could participate in decisionmaking. Land was usually held communally, and women, as they do today, played a major role in agricultural production. Under the French rule the effects of forced labor, commercial crop production, military recruitment, some Western education, and the relatively important, though small, wage-labor sectors enhanced the position of some men with

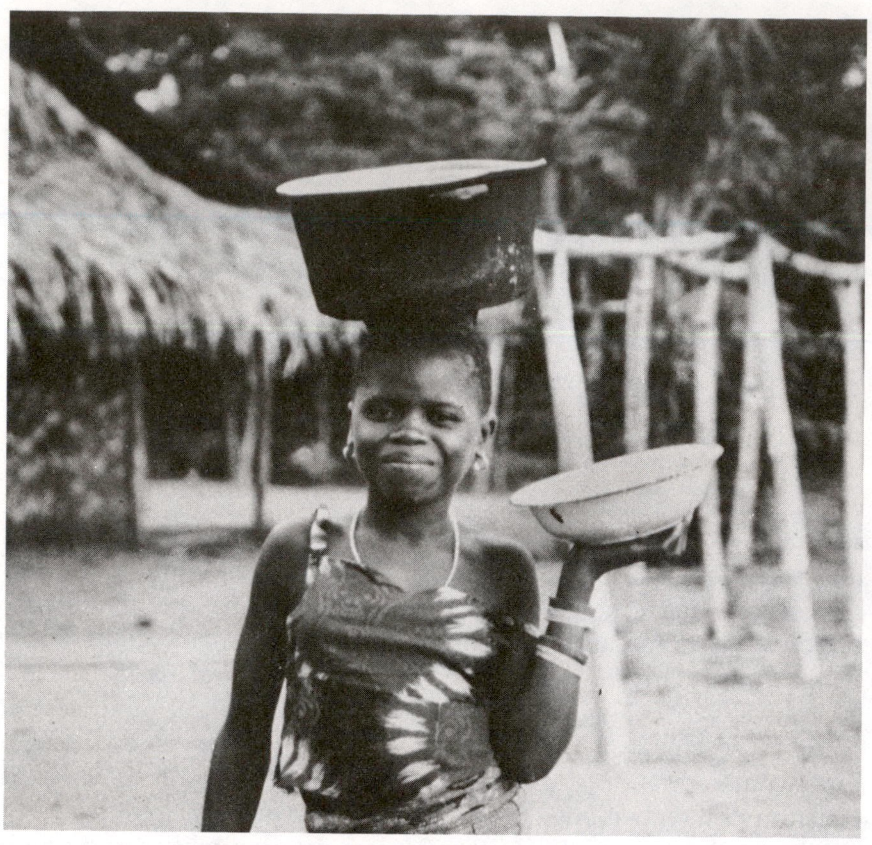

A young woman takes food to her husband. Photo courtesy of Barry Hewlett.

a consequent decline in the status of women. Excluded from wage labor, forbidden the right of divorce, and barred from the ownership of private property, women found themselves on the periphery of the European economy, at best increasingly dependent on males, at worst transformed into a dispossessed class. It became increasingly difficult for them to meet their own survival needs and those of their children. Of course in many rural areas the impact of the Western monetary economy was so small that it played virtually no part in the lives of most Central Africans, men or women. Independence in 1960 did little to alter this state of affairs.

For most women migration to the city was, from the beginning, more of an end in itself than it had been for men, who went mainly to obtain work. Until the late 1950s there was a tendency for Central African rural communities to retain their female members as virtual hostages for the return of the men. In the past thirty years, more women either accompanied their husbands or joined them later. As fewer young men remained in the villages and marriages become more difficult to arrange, increasing numbers of unmarried girls and women left their families for regional towns and the shantytowns of Bangui. Whether lured by the hope of an easier life or by the town's reputation as an exciting place, more and more women have joined the men as a "floating population," neither rural nor involved in wage employment.

A small number of Central African women have succeeded in obtaining a Western education. A handful have found positions in the administration, or as teachers, nurses, and shop assistants. Others have been able to obtain employment as service and industrial workers. The overwhelming majority of urban Central African women, though, trade in the market, sell illicit manioc alcohol, sell food from their homes, or subsist mainly by rendering sexual services for a fee. Even those few Central African women who are married to or related in some way to the new class of elite and high-ranking African bureaucratic bourgeoisie find that Central African men still tend to think of educated women as troublesome, critical, demanding, insubordinate, and neglectful of them and their children. With remarkedly few exceptions most Central African men, whether Western-educated or not, would agree with the Central African proverb, "The hen must never crow in the presence of the rooster."

The great majority of urban women probably find it more difficult to feed, clothe, house, and nurture their children than they did in the rural setting. Yet if one penetrates beneath the simplistic dichotomies of urban and rural, modern and traditional, still found in much of the literature on African women and urbanization, and if one makes direct contact with women living in individual *kodros,* one begins to sense a strength and resilience missed by the casual observer. By entering into the daily life and rhythm of a given *kodro,* one can perhaps find that very positive rural sociopolitical patterns still exist.

For example, in one specific *kodro,* Boy-Rabe, on the northern perimeter of Bangui, active women's organizations cultivate large fields of manioc that they make into flour, fried doughcakes, and alcohol to sell in front of their houses or in the Boy-Rabe market. The existence, resilience, and viability of these women's organizations are among the major factors that permit Bangui's continuance; without women's gardens in open spaces throughout the city Bangui would starve.

EDUCATION

During the colonial period the administration sought to avoid producing either a liberally educated intelligentsia that might become a focus for anticolonialist dissatisfaction or a well-trained group that might compete with French technicians.[13] Rather it sought to produce enough practically trained primary school graduates to serve the needs of the administration and commerce as auxiliaries to the Europeans and as intermediaries between them and the vast majority of nonliterate and non-French-speaking Africans. Until 1953 the only secondary education in Central Africa was through the missions, although from the mid-1930s there was an attempt to increase education opportunities for the most gifted through government subsidies to Protestant as well as Catholic mission schools and a few state schools. In general all Central African schools, until the late 1940s, remained poorly equipped and staffed largely by semiliterate African monitors. in 1953 the first secondary school, Collège Emil Gentil, was established and the first *baccalauréat* students graduated in 1956. By the 1957–1958 school year the territory that was to become the Central African Republic was devoting 19.3 percent of its budget to education, and 45,774 students were in primary school and 1,044 in secondary and technical schools.

At the time of independence only a handful of Central Africans had graduated from secondary school. Presidents Boganda and Dacko gave a high priority to scholastic development and by the 1965–1966 school year there were 128,436 students in primary schools, and 3,340 students in secondary and technical schools. Most adult Central Africans today, however, remain illiterate. About 50 percent of the school age population attend at least some primary school. A law passed on May 16, 1962, unified all Central African schools into a single system. The government declared

Educated young people are the hope of the CAR. Photo courtesy of Thomas O'Toole.

that it would assume full responsibility for the buildings, salaries of African personnel, and other operating expenses. European and U.S. missionaries who remained as teachers in the schools contributed their services. The establishment of the single school system took place with the consent of both Catholic and Protestant authorities under the auspices of the Dacko regime, which, as heir of Barthélemy Boganda, favored the mission presence in education. Because the financially strapped Central African government has been able to give less and less support to the increasingly crowded schools, the number of trained teachers and the amount of teaching materials have diminished. Over the past twenty years the level of instruction has declined steadily.

On paper there are presently more than 170,000 pupils attending about 780 primary schools, which have upwards of 2,600 teachers. The government claims that more than 10,000 students are attending some 20 secondary schools in which almost 400 teachers are employed. The University of Bangui, founded by Jean-Bedel Bokassa in 1967, has been operating fitfully since October 1970. The university was founded by Bokassa in direct opposition to French advice, and the first-year class in law and economics began without a regular fulltime faculty. Science and letters were added in 1971 along with an *Ecole Normale Supérieure* (teachers' college) and a University Institute of Mines and Geology. After the Soviet Union gave aid and personnel for the sciences, and Romania for geology and mines, the French reluctantly agreed to provide aid and personnel for the rest of the university; by 1979 the various institutions were largely French staffed and had more than 500 students. At present, in addition to the National School of Administration, the School of Arts and Crafts, the Medical School, and the National School of Agriculture (originally established in 1963), the rather confused system does offer a very uneven level of postsecondary instruction to those who have enough political pull to gain access.

The best students and especially those with the best political connections continue to go directly to France for higher education. The best teachers leave the classroom for better paying and more prestigious positions in the government. Teachers with less training are appointed to handle ever larger classes, and the quality of instruction at all levels continues to decline while the cost increases. The exclusive use of French as the language of instruction at the secondary and university level and the maintenance of largely unadapted French programs also contribute to the high rate of failure, repeating, and dropouts at all levels. Already uprooted by historical circumstances, Central African young people are further alienated from their environment by a school system that does little to prepare them to be responsible citizens or productive workers. The French-derived education system continues to create a parasitic group who seek to be supported by public funds and an even larger "lumpen bourgeoisie" of semiliterate failures whose single dream is government employment. The political turbulence of this latter group has been especially evident in Central Africa since they began the process that led to the French overthrow of Bokassa. The virtual absence of a private sector and the inability of the government to continue absorbing the growing numbers of ever more poorly educated secondary and university graduates are major factors of political unrest in the Central African Republic. If social and economic development is ever going to become a reality for the CAR, a more appropriate educational system will have to be developed and subsidized.

THE ARTS

Little of the vast array of sculpture in wood, stone, and cast metal—which has become a major African contribution to the world's museums and galleries—comes from the Central African Republic. The explorers Georg Schweinfurth, Wilhelm Junker, and Auguste Chevalier noted the existence of handmade textiles in the eastern part of the country at the end of the nineteenth century, and the Banda produced a wide variety of iron tools and weapons in the same period. The making of pottery, woven mats, leatherwork, and musical instruments was also well developed throughout the area. Apparently the disruption caused by the slave trade and the early years of colonization led to the disappearance of most of this craft industry. Some rather plain woven mats, baskets, and wooden utensils are about all the local handiwork to be found in the country today. Fulbé women who have moved into the *kodros* on Bangui's periphery in recent years produce some handshaped pottery. Little is of great artistic merit and most is of inferior technical quality as well.

One of the major art forms that does flourish in the Central African Republic today is popular music. A number of original dance bands are continually being formed and regrouped in Bangui and some of the regional towns. These groups, using modern Western instruments and sophisticated electronic equipment, play a wide variety of music. Faithfully reproducing Western pop music, rhythm and blues, and *rasta* music from the Caribbean as well as Zairian and other African regional music, they offer excellent performances. Under garish colored lights in open-air night spots like "Merci Maman," "La Luciole," "L'Etoile," and "La Dignité" in Kilometre Cinq, the best modern groups such as *Makembe, Musiki, Los Negritos,* and *Ngombeka* produce original music with a specifically Central African flavor. This music, with its haunting, melancholic vocals on a strong polyrhythmic base, has the potential of attracting international attention. Along with a strong and persisting tradition of ethnic dance, the urban dance-hall music of the Central African Republic would seem to be one of the most creative elements in Central Africa's artistic culture.

Written literature from the Central African Republic is not widely known. The local languages other than Sango have seldom been used in written form and few Central Africans have published works in French.[14] Of this handful by far the most original writer is Pierre Makombo Bamboté whose *Funeral Chants for an African Hero,* published in 1962, was filled with potential. The appearance ten years later of *Princess Mandapu* marked Bamboté as the foremost interpeter of Central African life as well as a major creative talent. Offering the reader an interesting blend of history, melodrama, and sociopolitical criticism, *Princess Mandapu* evokes Central African realities in a way that simple narrative cannot. Bamboté's 1981 collection of short stories, *News of Bangui,* continued to exhibit his artistry. A substantial oral literature of stories and proverbs exists in local languages as well, but little of this is available in written form. Four short stories by Faustin-Albert Ipeko-Etomane, in *The Lake of Sorcerers,* touch on some of these traditional legends, but considerable work in collection and editing of folk literature remains to be done throughout the Central African Republic.

A recent film produced with French government support by Central African–born Joseph Akoussoné, entitled *Zo Kwe Zo,* though not of major artistic value, is worthy of note as a history of the Central African Republic based partially on oral sources. The title in Sango is a quote from Barthélemy Boganda and means "a man is a man" or "all humans have a right to their proper dignity." The film begins with the creation of the French post at Bangui by Albert Dolisie and proceeds to the division of the country by concessionary companies, the beginnings of forced labor, and the development of cotton, coffee, and rubber plantations. The film goes on to evoke the participation of Central Africans in the two world wars, the Brazzaville conference, and the independence movement. Hardly an objective historical film even with the technical assistance of the Zairian, Elikia M'Bokolo, director of the Zairian *Centre d'Etudes Africaines, Zo Kwe Zo* is important as a first attempt by a Central African to produce films with a Central African viewpoint. Its rather cavalier treatment of facts, documents, and available photos combined with a gossipy approach does have the benefit of rendering it accessible to more Central Africans than if it were a more formal social history. Perhaps Akouissonné and other Central African cinematographers may one day create films about the Central African Republic that will rival those of Ousmane Sembene in Senegal.

Painting in the Central African Republic is far from a recent phenomenon. Rock paintings in caves east of Ndélé, for example, may be as old as any in sub-Saharan Africa.[15] Though very difficult to document, it is likely that a tradition of decorative painting on the mud-walls of houses, today much in decline, has also existed for generations.

In more than one instance this tradition has been transferred to water colors, oil, and gouache. In Fort Sibut, Jerome Ramedané, a former farmer based near Kaga Bandoro, has created a whole series of wall paintings and canvases depicting scenes of wild animals, hunts, and daily life that have a remarkable naive vigor and originality. Similar works, though often not as notable, are sometimes found on walls of bars and restaurants in Bangui and regional towns.[16]

A small cottage industry of highly repetitious and stylized sketches of village life on note paper and cotton table sets in pen and ink and oil has also been created. This production for tourists and international visitors grows out of mission-school craft classes that also developed a form of decorative art in which brilliantly colored butterfly wings are glued together in abstract and representational designs. A few producers of these works create unique and original compositions.

NOTES

1. The treatment of ethnicity offered here generally follows Dennis D. Cordell, "The Savanna Belt of North-Central Africa," in *History of Central Africa,* Vol. 1, ed. David Birmingham and Phyllis M. Martin (London: Longman, 1983), 30–74.

2. Pierre Kalck, *Central African Republic: A Failure in De-Colonization,* trans. Barbara Thomson (New York: Praeger, 1971), 29.

3. See Joseph H. Greenberg, *The Languages of Africa* (Bloomington: Indiana University Research Center in Anthropology, Folklore, and Linguistics, 1963).

4. Eugene V. Rosenau, ed. *Sango-English Dictionary 1980* (Cleveland: Baptist Mid-Missions, 1980), xi–xii.

5. This two-part linguistic explanation owes much to Cordell, *The Savanna Belt.*

6. In Central Africa this term is applied to all Arabicized Africans from the north whether or not they are actually Hausa.

7. *Quarterly Economic Review of Gabon, Congo, Cameroon, Central African Republic, Chad, and Equatorial Guinea,* annual supplement (London: The Economist Intelligence Unit, Ltd., 1983), 35.

8. These figures from the 1970s are based on Gérard Grellet, Monique Mainguet, and Pierre Soumille, *La République Centrafricaine* (Paris: Presses Universitaires de France, 1982), 97–99.

9. Much of this discussion on *kodros* is based on personal observation and Marie-France Adrien-Rongier, "Les Kodro de Bangui: Un espace urbain 'oublié,'" *Cahiers d'etudes Africaines* 21 (1981), 43–110.

10. This discussion of the subjective viewpoints of urban dwellers is based on the author's personal observations and conversations conducted during a nine-month period from October 1979 through June 1980.

11. These observations are based upon informal conversations of the author and faculty colleagues with students at the University of Bangui, October 1979 through June 1980, and more extensive interviews and conversations conducted by a number of Peace Corps teachers between August 1979 and October 1983. Individual letters to the author from a number of former students also contribute to these observations.

12. Unpublished paper, "From Independence to Dependence: The Food Situation in the Central African Republic," by Dr. Claude Chauvigné, Department of Romance Languages, University of North Carolina-Greensboro, Greensboro, N.C., 1981.

13. Material in this section is drawn from personal observation and correspondence; see also David E. Gardiner, "Schooling in the States of Equatorial Africa," *Canadian Journal of African Studies* 8 (1974), 517–538.

14. For bibliographic details on works cited here see Hans Zell, Carol Bundy, and Virginia Coulon, eds., *A New Reader's Guide to African Literature* (New York: Africana Publishing Co., 1983), 277–278.

15. Grellet et al., *La République Centrafricaine,* 54.

16. Yvan Audouard, "Le Jour de Gloire de Jerome Ramedané," *Balafon* (July 1979), 16–21.

5

Economic and Political Dependence

Anger and sadness are constant companions of those who examine the political economy of the Central African Republic over the past century. What is most frustrating is the virtual absence of any improvement in the quality of life for most Central Africans. From its first involvement with the world capitalist economy in the slave trade through the imposition of formal control by European powers and into the present, the Central African Republic has a history marked by an erosion of village economies and a decline in meeting the basic human needs[1] of most Central Africans. As the involvement of the Republic in the world economic system grew, so did the degree of inequality within the society. Political decolonization and independence have not benefited the majority of the people of Central Africa.

ECONOMICS

Against a background of increased economic and technological dependence, Central African political leadership has played little, if any, positive role in solving problems of mass poverty and increasing unemployment. Like more than a dozen other African countries, the Central African Republic is both absolutely and relatively poorer than most of the rest of the world. Whether judged in terms of per capita gross national product (GNP) or on the basis of a "quality of life" index,[2] the CAR, despite its relatively small population and considerable resource base, is one of the world's poorest countries. The outlook for the immediate future holds little hope of improvement for the majority of the country's population. The GNP per head in 1985 was put at $310 by the World Bank, and over the period since independence it is estimated to have grown at an average annual rate of no more than 0.6 percent. The gross domestic product (GDP) per capita of $300 in 1982 has since fallen by more than 2.3 percent because population has risen faster than the GDP has grown. There are perhaps 140,000 wage and salary earners and of this number at least 80,000 are in government service. Only 35,000 people, at most, are employed in the industrial sector. Much of the rural population, by far the majority of Central Africans, lives mainly at the subsistence and small-scale homestead level and does not even enter into most GNP figures.

The study of economics in Africa was dominated until the mid-1970s by liberal theories of development and accommodation to a world market. These theories stressed economic growth as a means to overcome poverty. From this perspective the present situation in the CAR is quite easily explained. Principal among the factors accounting for the country's continuing political and economic difficulties have been chronic and ever-growing government deficits and mismanagement of the country's key export-earning economic activities. The small Central African urban-centered elite, or bureaucratic bourgeoisie, factions of which have jockeyed for political control in Bangui since the early 1950s, has by training and conditioning evolved consumption, lifestyle, and vacation patterns that tie it to France. Largely alienated from the indigenous society, this co-opted urban elite has become the rather inept political administrators of a neocolonial state. Since independence, the steady growth of the public sector, the continued expansion of government expenditures for administration, and the spiraling costs of maintaining this African bourgeoisie[3] at ever higher levels of luxury have drained off what little direct investment capital might have been available after most profits have been expatriated. Since independence, lacking any other means of legitimization of their rule, the bureaucratic bourgeoisie has used administrative appointments as a spoils system to reward kin and lineage supporters. Consequently, the civil service in the Central African Republic has swelled until it now absorbs more than 80 percent of the budget.

More radical analysts maintain that economic conditions like those in the Central African Republic also have deeper structural causes that transcend internal difficulties within the country.[4] From this perspective the predominance of France and other Western nations in virtually all areas of economic endeavor has locked the Republic into a condition of underdevelopment. For those who argue from this dependency viewpoint, the basic obstacle to economic development in the CAR remains the persistent, parasitical subservience of the Central African economy to French and other Western entrepreneurs and commercial interests. This fundamental political obstacle to equitable economic development would have to be removed before the equally formidable generic difficulties facing the nation could be adequately challenged. The economic ineptness of the present Central African leadership is, from this perspective, simply a symptom of the deeper structural problems of dependency. More than twenty-five years after political independence of French political influence, economic preponderance, and cultural conditioning cannot be overcome without a radical challenge to the current neocolonial situation.

POLITICAL ECONOMY UNDER COLONIALISM

Making landlocked Ubangi-Shari profitable was not easy at the beginning of the twentieth century. With the decline of the trade in ivory and the end of the slave trade, the collection of wild rubber from the roots of a number of different plant species became the major source of wealth. The commerce in wild rubber was almost exclusively a monopoly of French concessionaires who were given a free hand in exploiting local labor. Local food production declined by more than 50 percent as whole villages were uprooted and relocated to collect wild rubber in ever more remote areas and villagers themselves often fled into the bush to avoid forced labor.

In the early 1930s when rubber prices fell and the wild sources were used up, the French colonial administration introduced cotton production as a means of generating an export commodity. With no fertilizer and rudimentary tools production was never very high. Furthermore, cotton transportation and marketing was left in the hands of French and other foreign intermediaries who offered such low prices to the Central African growers that only the increased demands for cash tax payments by the colonial administration could force Central Africans to grow cotton at all. While a greater demand and hence marginally higher prices for cotton and even wild rubber caused some increase in production during World War II, few Central Africans were willing to be exploited for the benefit of French commercial interests.

After World War II Ubangi-Shari, as part of the federation of *Afrique Equatoriale Française* (AEF), was even more directly tied to the French economy. From 1947 to 1959 Ubangi-Shari received 8,603,400,000 CFA francs for economic development from the French government. Certain AEF institutions and a coordinated development plan were used to attempt to integrate AEF development, but this coordination consisted largely of setting production targets to meet the demands of the French market. A stabilization fund was established in 1955 to ensure some price stability for Central Africa's major export crops: cotton, peanuts, and coffee. A system of collective credit, processing facilities, and institutions to modernize production and develop agricultural infrastructure was also established, but few Central Africans had the knowledge or initial capital necessary to gain access to these institutions. French and other foreign entrepreneurs were able to borrow capital, employ better techniques, and benefit from these new institutions, but small-scale African producers faced declining production and increasingly lower prices as a result. French private mercantile and commercial firms and companies such as Peyrissac, Chawanel, and others monopolized the purchase of cash crops so that small African producers were forced to sell at whatever price they were offered. French and other foreign intermediaries even traded in subsistence crops. Collecting inflated payment in kind for imported necessities, these dealers would store the food crops and sell them back at a large markup to African producers later in the year when supplies ran out.

Although goods theoretically circulated freely within the AEF, most Central African trade was an unequal flow of low-priced raw materials to France in exchange for high-priced French manufactured goods. The protective policies made possible by a common external tariff for the AEF never operated to harmonize and coordinate production for the benefit of Central Africans. Rather than creating local industries, French commercial interests encouraged direct bilateral links with Paris. Instead of investing in the production of basic consumer goods in Ubangi-Shari, French and other foreign merchants simply imported and sold mostly French goods at inflated prices in return for local cash crops purchased at low prices from small African producers who could not control the market. The foreign mercantile groups were thus able to reap a relatively high return with very little capital investment.

The 1956 *Loi-Cadre* added a greater political autonomy for each AEF territory to the already existing economic balkanization. De Gaulle's draft constitution of 1958 ended the federal structure of the AEF and reinforced direct links between the French government and each of the AEF territories, including Ubangi-Shari. The Ubangi-Shari assembly did, though, have to consult Brazzaville on all development plans financed by FIDES (*Fonds d'Investissement pour le Développement Economique et Social*), which were financed by French public funds. French government price supports for Central African coffee and cotton paid an increased dividend to French commercial interests, though the benefits of these price supports never reached the small African producers who were forced to sell at low prices to French and other foreign intermediaries. French aid and technical support were also an absolute necessity to the African bureaucratic bourgeoisie, which was to inherit the political leadership of the Central African Republic. With no real source of revenue other than that obtained from French government subsidies and import-export taxes, the government of the CAR had to accept the constitution of the Fifth French Republic and the neocolonial economic system that went with it.

POSTINDEPENDENCE POLITICAL ECONOMY

After independence the Central African Republic continued to depend on foreign aid for almost all of its development programs.[5] France was by far the largest supplier of this financial aid, supplying 1,215,400,000 CFA francs in 1960, as well as other forms of aid either directly or indirectly, such as the salaries of more than 400 French technical assistants, the transfer of staff, research expenses,

Table 5.1
Budget deficits in billions of CFA francs

	1979	1980	1981	1982	1983	1984
Expenditures	24.5	26.1	26.0	38.2	44.1	48.1
Deficits	--	--	14.0	8.0	7.8	9.5

Sources: *Marchés Tropicaux et Mediterranéens*, *Agri-Afrique*, *FAO Production Yearbook*, *Tropical Products Quarterly*, *IMF International Financial Statistics*, *IMF Direction of Trade Statistics*, and *The Economist Intelligence Unit Quarterly Economic Review of Gabon, Congo, Cameroon, Central African Republic, Chad, Equatorial Guinea*. Figures are, at best, approximations because statistics from the CAR are often not reliable.

subsidies for textile plants, and sowing bonuses for the larger planters (who were usually French or other Europeans). The French also supplied what would become inevitable subsidies to balance the budget (See Table 5.1). In 1960, total French aid exceeded 3,000,000,000 CFA francs, a sum equivalent to the total of the country's exports. This state of affairs, with minor fluctuations, has persisted to the present. In March 1959 FIDES was replaced by the *Fonds d'Aide et Coopération* (FAC), which continued to be financed and operated in the same ways as FIDES. As an associated overseas state of the European Economic Community (EEC) through its ties with France, the Central African Republic was to have free access to the EEC markets for coffee while France gradually dismantled its price-support system. Rather than participate in the development of strong regional economic organization, the CAR came to rely on France and the EEC for markets and development aid. Meanwhile, deterioration of terms of trade for coffee and cotton continued to create greater deficits in the Central African Republic's balance of payments with France and the EEC.

The Central African Republic did, however, join the *Union Africaine et Malgache* (UAM), created in 1960 to promote Francophone interests and to try to achieve a unified approach to matters of common economic concern. The Central African Republic also joined the *Organisation Commune Africaine et Malgache* (OCAM), which replaced UAM in 1965.[6] In economic terms neither of these two organizations proved of major importance to the Central African Republic.

The *Union Douanière et Economique de l'Afrique Centrale* (UDEAC) was created in 1966 by the five neighboring former French territories in Equatorial Africa: Cameroon, Chad, Congo, Gabon, and the Central African Republic. Its function was to harmonize taxation and tariff policies among member states by prohibiting the levying of customs or fiscal duties. Its purpose was also to rationalize investment codes, development plans, telecommunications, social legislation, and fiscal policies. Though never realizing its most grandiose plans, UDEAC did render considerable service to the CAR, especially in facilitating access to the sea through its neighboring states of Cameroon, Congo, and Gabon.

On October 18, 1983, the Central African Republic and nine other Central African nations signed a treaty in Libreville, Gabon, creating the *Communauté Economique des Etats de l'Afrique Centrale* (CEEAC). Joining together members of the UDEAC with three former Belgian territories, Burundi, Rwanda, and Zaire, a former Spanish colony, Equatorial Guinea, and a former Portuguese colony, Sao Tomé and Principe, the CEEAC seeks to strengthen existing subregional cooperation. It also reaffirms the commitment of the Organization of African Unity (OAU) to a continentwide economic community and a common market by the year 2000. Based on the Economic Commission for Africa of the United Nations and OAU plans evolved in the late 1970s, the long-range goal of this and other such regional groupings in Africa is to promote economic and industrial cooperation among member states. It is assumed that UDEAC will merge into the CEEAC to avoid costly duplication of services. Whether or not CEEAC will be able gradually to remove trade restrictions among these states and establish a common external tariff remains open to question. In any case, major benefits of the CEEAC to Central Africa would seem quite distant: The Central African Republic will receive little assistance in solving the immediate problem of balancing the national budget. For the present, the country remains directly tied to France for this assistance.

The strongest link between France and the Central African Republic is the franc zone. After independence in 1960, the Central African Republic joined with Cameroon, Chad, Congo, Gabon, and Madagascar in the reformed monetary arrangement offered by the franc zone, including a share in the French-controlled central bank, the *Banque Centrale des Etats de l'Afrique Centrale* (BCEAC), which issues a common currency, the *Communauté Financière Africaine* (CFA) franc. Under the franc zone system, the CFA currency is freely convertible to the French franc at a fixed exchange rate (50 CFA francs = 1 French franc).

Furthermore, the French Ministry of Finance retains a representative on the governing board of the bank and, though the headquarters is now in Yaoundé rather than Paris, the reserves are still held in French francs. All the exchange transactions are handled by the French Treasury. The Central African Republic thus has a currency that is readily exchangeable on world money markets, but the country cannot control totally its external reserves or the credit policies of French commercial banks operating in Central Africa. A common currency has not stimulated CFA member states to coordinate their economic and social development or establish a full customs union. Dependent on permission of the French treasury to draw on reserves for capital investment, the CAR has never had enough capital to attempt long-range social and economic investment plans.

PLANNING AND ECONOMIC AID

It is perhaps symptomatic of global inequality and dependence that states like the Central African Republic that most need better planning tend to have the least. Central Africa needs the best possible future studies to master its own destiny, yet, perhaps as a direct result of its French colonial heritage, the phenomenon of centralized economic development planning has gained currency among the CAR bureaucratic bourgeoisie. From the total failure of Guérillot's ambitious production-based development plans under Boganda, through the collapse of Dacko's even more grandiose development schemes and the ultimate debacle of Bokassa's development projects, to the grand pronouncements of Kolingba, one theme remained constant. The leaders of Central Africa, along with their French and other foreign advisers, continued to seek economic development through a centrally controlled "productionist" approach without any attempt to consult with the small agriculturalists who are the basic producers in this overwhelmingly agricultural economy. The only benefactors for this persistence in the face of failure are the planners themselves and those who supply the spate of imported goods and technical assistance with which each new centrally planned project is launched. The Plan tends to acquire an independent reality and substitutes for actual work in the real world instead of being an instrument to aid the economy.

Given the absolute as well as the relative lack of investment capital, historically a problem in the Central African Republic, all development plans to date have operated under the assumption that growth requires foreign trade, foreign investment, and an international demand for Central African exports. The limitations of import substitutions industries that are highly dependent on imported materials, technology, and foreign ownership is all too apparent. Yet the Kolingba government, like those that preceded it, continues to rely upon national development schemes based on export-led growth.

The Five Year Plan for 1986–1990, developed under French guidance, recites a litany similar to that of most Francophone African countries. It calls for increased development of exportable agricultural products, additional expenditures for technical and managerial training, greater infrastructure and expenditures, and better health care. The whole plan assumes that the French will continue their major $38.6 million yearly aid and that other donors will be forthcoming. It also clearly rests on the following assumptions: growing external demands for Central African products, comparative advantage, a continuing neocolonial institutional framework characterized by the production of raw material for export under foreign entrepreneurship, and capital. This long-term plan is fundamentally dependent upon the growth of the French economy because there is little likelihood of other major new markets for Central African exports. Unfortunately, given these major constraints, export proceeds cannot be expected to grow at the same rate as the urban elite's propensity to import automobiles, household durables, processed food, and large and often inappropriate mechanical equipment. The plan's unrealistic projections condemn the Central African Republic to a continuing shortage of foreign exchange and a growing deficit in the country's balance of payments. This shortage is, and will continue to be, aggravated by the leakage of funds through capital and wage repatriation from the more than 400 French *coopérants* currently working in the Central African Republic and by French control of the banking system.

In the early months of Kolingba's regime there were some hopeful signs that a new era in relations between France and the CAR, as well as a new approach to economic and social development, might be at hand. Appointing Abel Goumba, virtually the only Central African political figure with an unblemished record with regard to corruption, as rector of the University of Bangui, Kolingba seemed to be establishing a new direction for Central African development. The national secretary of the French Socialist party, Lionel Jospin, voiced strong support for Goumba's statements about economic and political self-reliance for the Central African Republic. Goumba's view that the solution to the country's problems must be found by Central Africans was certainly heartening. The long-term pro-African stance of Mitterrand and his government[7] might have led to a sustained program of infusion of subsidies for at least a generation without subjecting the CAR to greater neocolonial control. This, of course, was all predicated on a new Central African government staffed by decent, hardworking, self-sufficient, and trained people. Kolingba's reversion to the now familiar Central African patterns of personalized authoritarian rule put an end to any movement in that direction by early 1983. In spite of the avowed hostility to French military intervention in Africa originally claimed by President Mitterrand, the continued presence of French commandos in the Central African Republic is a constant reminder that most of the country's actions are still predicated on decisions made in the Elysée Palace.

From de Gaulle's continued "special relationship" with Africa through Giscard d'Estaing's personal relationship with Central African rulers to the Mitterand government's continued hegemony, however reluctant, France's vital economic interests have been preserved. This overwhelming French presence is often justified by the French in terms of Central Africa's strategic position in the continent or the country's uranium reserves. It would appear, though, that the clear economic benefits to French business and private interests are sufficient causes for the relatively unwavering French policy toward the CAR over the past twenty-five years.

In fact, in spite of some lip service to the effect that generosity toward the Third World is consistent with French interest, the policies of Mitterrand's Socialist government toward Central Africa differ little from those of Giscard d'Estaing.

The stated policy of the Mitterrand government from mid-1981 was that aid to the Central African Republic should come not only from governmental agencies and multinational companies but also from trade unions, municipalities, and professional bodies. Moreover, under Mitterrand the Ministry of Cooperation was charged with assisting small and medium-sized French companies to play a larger role in French aid efforts. Emphasizing increased French research on Africa, the improvement of agriculture, joint ventures in industrial development, and a greater emphasis on improved health care, the Mitterrand economic development package for Central Africa is remarkably similar to that of the preceding government. In fact President Mitterrand seems to have begun his term in office thinking he would restore French prestige and power in international relations by becoming the leader of a third force that would include France and Third World countries, especially those from Francophone Africa.

By the end of Kolingba's first year in power, the African leader was praised in Paris by Mitterrand's foreign minister, Claude Cheysson, at a state dinner held in Kolingba's honor and, for all practical purposes, the neocolonial tutelage that had been the hallmark of relations between France and the Central African Republic was never displaced. The brief rupture that had followed the brief asylum of the opposition leader, Ange Patassé, in the French embassy in Bangui after a supposed attempt on March 3, 1982, had given way to a *realpolitik* that differed little from the Gaullist line in operation since independence. Given that French managers dominate the banks and that French investors own most of the country's industry, it is little wonder that a strong domestic lobby in France supports a continued presence in this otherwise unimportant country.

SPECIFIC AREAS OF CONCERN

One of the major constraints to economic growth in the Central African Republic continues to be the nation's landlocked status. Because all import and export products must pass through seaports that are either 1,400 kilometers (Douala, Cameroon) or 1,800 kilometers (Pointe-Noire, Congo) away from Bangui, any economic change must contend with this difficulty for both imports and exports. All external trade is dependent upon the goodwill of the United Republic of Cameroon and the Popular Republic of the Congo. The river transportation system, linked by rail to the sea from Brazzaville to Pointe-Noire, carries 65 percent of all imports and exports. Yet continuing managerial and financial problems, deteriorated equipment, declining export traffic volume, drought that lowers river levels, and silting contribute to a major external transportation crisis for the country.

Internal transportation fares little better. With the exception of some recently completed segments of the Trans-African highway, the route from Nola to Bouar, and the roads leading directly out of Bangui, the majority of the roads in the Central African Republic are in a very dilapidated state. The road network of some 22,000 kilometers has less than 500 hard-surfaced kilometers. The 4,950-kilometer national road system is poorly maintained and many of the more than 14,000 kilometers of unmaintained rural feeder roads are often little more than tracks through the forest or across the open savanna. At the height of the rainy season most road traffic in the country ceases altogether.

This lack of adequate farm-to-market roads has a direct bearing on the nation's political stability. Meeting the food needs of Bangui's exploding population becomes ever more difficult as it becomes necessary to go increasingly far afield to gather the scattered produce of this agriculturally backward country. Most livestock is herded to market rather than trucked, with a subsequent loss of time, weight, and quality. Access north into the livestock- and grain-producing areas of Chad is limited by the deteriorated condition of the main roads to Sarh and N'Djamena. The road east into the potentially productive valleys from Bangui to Obo near the border with Sudan and Zaire is scarcely passable during much of the year, and river transportation to Ouango in the east through the potentially fruitful Ubangi valley has declined in recent years due to inadequate maintenance of facilities and equipment. Only the rich fruit, vegetable, and coffee-producing areas around

A portion of the Trans-African highway in the CAR. Photo courtesy of Thomas O'Toole.

Nola on the Sangha River are still served by boat on a more or less reliable schedule.

Road and river transportation has become so unreliable and difficult that parts of the country distant from Bangui have come to depend on private air transport for imported foodstuffs. This method is, of course, too costly and rare for most people and is effectively available to only a few people, chiefly resident aliens, who can afford it.

The only international airport accessible to commercial aircraft is the Bangui-M'Poko Airport just outside Bangui. From this airport direct passenger and freight service to most neighboring countries is available. Air Afrique, UTA, and Le Point provide regular air service from France to Bangui as well.

Qualified and trained managers and technicians of all sorts are the second major infrastructure need in the Central African Republic. For a variety of historical, cultural, and perhaps nutritional factors, Central Africa lacks personnel trained in the necessary managerial, planning, analysis, and administrative functions to create, direct, and upgrade agricultural, manufacturing, trade, and marketing institutions for the nation. A relatively large number of Central Africans who have been educated as scientists, tech-

Table 5.2
Gross domestic product by sector in billions of CFA francs

	1980	1981	1982	1983	1984	1985
Agriculture, forestry, and fishing	62.1	69.2	73.9	72.3	70.1	69.8
Manufacturing	14.0	16.0	19.6	17.5	17.3	16.6
Mining	13.1	11.5	13.5	13.5	13.3	12.9
Public services	25.9	31.3	35.2	34.3	34.5	34.6
Private services	17.6	20.6	23.8	24.1	25.2	24.0

Sources: *Marchés Tropicaux et Mediterranéens*, *Agri-Afrique*, *FAO Production Yearbook*, *Tropical Products Quarterly*, *IMF International Financial Statistics*, *IMF Direction of Trade Statistics*, and *The Economist Intelligence Unit Quarterly Economic Review of Gabon, Congo, Cameroon, Central African Republic, Chad, Equatorial Guinea*. Figures are, at best, approximations because statistics from the CAR are often not reliable.

nologists, and specialists of all kinds have chosen to remain abroad, discouraged by the uncongenial and unsettled conditions at home. Far too few of the most talented and best educated Central Africans have made any attempt to engage in productive and profit-making industrial, agricultural, or service pursuits. Most have sought to become part of a swollen and nonproductive civil service that continues to absorb most of the Republic's foreign exchange in luxury consumption without producing anything.

Agriculture is still the major activity of 80 percent of the nation's population, and yet it represents only 31 percent of the GDP (See Table 5.2). This is true in spite of the fact that somewhat less than 10 percent of the country's surface is good, arable soil and only about one-sixth of this is actually under cultivation. Most Central Africans still live in villages where self-sufficient agriculture is practiced within traditional slash-and-burn cultivation systems. Hunting and gathering, in many cases, remain more important than cultivation and are an indispensible source of food everywhere in the country. For most Central Africans the only meat eaten is wild game, with the rare exception of a semidomestic chicken or goat.

Although bananas in the forest zone, rice and maize in the southern savanna, and peanuts and millet in the northern savanna could furnish an adequate nutritional base for the country's rural population, most people are slowly starving on diets based on manioc (cassava). The transition from valuable food crops to a nonnutritional starchy root crop began in the first decades of the century when the forced production of cotton and coffee for export took away the time needed to grow better food crops. Manioc grows on marginal land with little care and hence of necessity became a major food source. This continues today in spite of the strong likelihood that the manioc, incompletely cooked over fires fed by hard-to-gather wood, deposits cyanide poisons in humans. This poison builds up over time, causing a variety of grave ills beginning with goiter, endemic in rural Central Africa. Other illnesses probably related to manioc consumption are especially harmful to young children. These illnesses also cause thyroid problems, premature senility, and general deterioration of the nervous system.

Using rather haphazard "slash-burn-cultivate-abandon" farming techniques that rely on rudimentary hand tools, chiefly the short-handled hoe, most Central African cultivators have very low crop yields. From their low income base these cultivators are unable to finance needed inputs such as improved seeds and work animals and, in most cases, lack the skills and training to benefit from most capital improvements. Substandard roads, which prevent development of good marketing networks, the absence of an agricultural credit system for the small producer, the absence of farmer cooperatives and a practically worthless government extension program for crops other than cotton characterize the present situation in Central African agricultural production.

The generally poor soils, occasional failure of the seasonal rains, and other difficulties of tropical African agriculture are compounded in the Republic by historically created social and cultural practices mitigating against optimum effort on the part of most cultivators. Virtually continual conflict and the ravages of both the trans-Saharan and the Atlantic slave trades had largely disrupted agriculture in the Central African Republic before the onset of colonial occupation. The majority of the population in the country's potentially most productive areas had given up any major effort to expand food-crop production. Retreating to the forest fringe, seeking the most secluded valleys, and constantly moving as danger threatened, almost all Central African people had regressed by the end of the nineteenth century to a basically hunting and gathering economy, cultivating only those staples that grew fairly rapidly and required a minimum of labor. French colonial exploitation with forced labor further dislocated these fragile societies and uprooted the few remaining stable villages. To date its postindependence governments have done little to reverse these negative effects, and at present the country faces a severe food-crop shortage.

Without adequate marketing and transportation resources, increased production of crucial domestic food crops like sorghum, peanuts, millet, rice, and sesame is unlikely to keep up with growing populations (See Table 5.3). In spite of this severe constraint the present government, under the guidance of the International Monetary Fund, the World Bank, and others in the international community, agreed to an ambitious plan to increase exports of coffee, cotton, and tobacco in order to achieve a better balance of trade (See Table 5.4).

Currently cotton is produced by some 280,000 planters, more than 90 percent of whom are found in savanna prefectures of Ouham, Ouham-Pendé, Ouaka, and Nemo-Gribingui. Until 1982 the state-owned *Union Cotonnière Centrafricaine* (UCC) monopolized this production with about 2,850 buying points, 20 gins, and 1 oil press. Following the practice of French and other foreign merchants, this government monopoly sought to squeeze out a profit by paying producers the lowest possible prices. The 28,000-metric-ton production levels recorded in the late 1970s did not meet the cotton needs of the country's own small textile industry. The 1981–1982 harvest of 7,000 tons of cotton lint represented a steady decline in production, which orthodox economists blamed on inadequate market incentives to plant cotton and poor management of the state-owned company.

Faced with a desperate need to seek ever more foreign funds, Kolingba was able to persuade the World Bank to grant the Central African Republic substantial loans in 1982. In order to accomplish this he had to accept a severe retrenchment of government expenses and a plan for increased production of export crops. Bowing to World Bank pressures, the Kolingba government acquiesced to the creation of a joint French and Central African Republic parastatal (mixed state and private enterprise) cotton company in 1983. This

Table 5.3
Estimated production of basic food crops (in thousands of tons)

	1976	1977	1978	1979	1980	1981	1982	1983	1984	1985
Millet & Sorghum	42	42	40	41	46	55	50	52	50	48
Manioc	850	900	940	970	920	900	1005	1008	1002	1007
Maize	42	33	30	39	41	46	40	38	35	39
Rice	12	18	16	18	20	12	16	14	13	11
Bananas & Plantains	131	134	136	120	139	166	146	152	149	147

Sources: *Marches Tropicaux et Mediterraneens*, *Agri-Afrique*, *FAO Production Yearbook*, *Tropical Products Quarterly*, *IMF International Financial Statistics*, *IMF Direction of Trade Statistics*, and *The Economist Intelligence Unit Quarterly Economic Review of Gabon, Congo, Cameroon, Central African Republic, Chad, Equatorial Guinea*. Figures are, at best, approximations because statistics from the CAR are often not reliable.

Table 5.4
Estimated production of main cash crops (in metric tons)

	1979/80	1980/81	1981/82	1982/83	1983/84	1984/85
Coffee	10,945	11,363	15,430	16,773	14,932	13,783
Cotton	38,180	28,940	23,756	37,300	45,493	42,627
Peanuts	86,000	120,000	123,000	125,000	128,000	127,529
Tobacco	1,800	1,189	1,038	706	699	1,806

Sources: *Marchés Tropicaux et Mediterranéens*, *Agri-Afrique*, *FAO Production Yearbook*, *Tropical Products Quarterly*, *IMF International Financial Statistics*, *IMF Direction of Trade Statistics*, and *The Economist Intelligence Unit Quarterly Economic Review of Gabon, Congo, Cameroon, Central African Republic, Chad, Equatorial Guinea*. Figures are, at best, approximations because statistics from the CAR are often not reliable.

organization sought to return cotton production to at least former levels and thus increase export earnings.

Following usual World Bank directions, this parastatal increased producer prices, retrenched unneeded processing facilities, and began improving the market and transportation networks. Forecasting a 60 percent increase in the first year of operation, the refinanced parastatal optimistically projected that cotton would account for more than 8 percent of the export earnings for the Central African Republic in the future. Its orthodox methods received self-fulfilling support from the fact that a substantial producer price increase (from 50 CFA francs to 80 CFA francs per kilogram of raw cotton) at the beginning of the 1984 planting season caused a one-time increase in the year's harvest to over 45,000 metric tons in spite of a severe drought. Without the same substantial subsidies the harvest will not long remain at this high level.

Unfortunately, as with so many "top-down" attempts to enhance production of export crops, the sociocultural resistance of Central African producers to cotton production was not taken into consideration. (Cotton remains in the eyes of most Central African producers a part of the colonial and postcolonial forced labor and concessionary system.) Given the growing food deficit in the cotton areas as well as elsewhere, it is unlikely that such simple market mechanisms as artificially raising producers' prices for a few years will convince small producers to plant very much more cotton.

The Central African Republic is listed by the United Nations Food and Agricultural Organization (FAO) as one of the twenty-four African countries with serious long-term food shortages. Cereal production fell from 103,000 metric tons in 1981 to about 88,000 metric tons in 1985. Marginal increases in cotton prices will be of little value if grain imports of 60,000 metric tons, of which only 9,000 are covered on concessional terms, force food prices to inflate. This is especially true as the CFA franc's purchasing power against the dollar is recovering only slowly.

Many of the same constraints facing increased cotton production exist for the production of coffee, the major commercial crop. Robusta coffee is cultivated in more than one-third of the country, but most coffee production is in the forest zone. Small-scale producers on about 23,000 hectares and a few larger-scale producers on somewhat less than 15,000 hectares produce, at best, as much as 17,000 metric tons per year. Here again marketing is overseen by a newly revitalized parastatal that has been active in stabilizing producer prices and reforming customs laws to combat the inevitable smuggling that such price stabilization efforts have engendered.

Production for the 1983–1984 and 1984–1985 seasons (the season runs from October to September) was lower than that for 1982–1983. The Central African government and its foreign advisors maintained that this decline in production was the result of drought and not of the indirect taxation effect of price stabilization. This drought explanation was an attempt to convince officials of the European Development Fund, the French assistance programs, and the African Development Bank, all active in promoting increased coffee production, that their investments were sound. The more likely explanation, not often considered by top-down development planners, is that small cultivators are simply behaving rationally and either devoting greater efforts to food production than to producing coffee more cheaply or selling more coffee in Cameroon where prices have been consistently higher. It is probably not coincidental that Cameroonian coffee production for the 1982–1983, 1983–1984 and 1984–1985 season was at all-time highs and that most of this increase was in robusta coffee from the eastern areas of the country, along the border with the Central African Republic.

Tobacco, which accounts for 5 percent of total export earnings, is produced on small family plots in the prefectures of Haute-Sangha, Basse-Kotto, and Mbomou. "Black" tobacco produced for cigars is most extensively cultivated, and although small cigar and cigarette enterprises in Bangui use 2 percent of the total commercialized production, most is shipped overland to Douala for export. The bulk goes to the European Economic Community with a very small part shipped to the United States for chewing tobacco. Tobacco marketing is handled by yet another joint French and Central African company.

The commercial production of other agricultural products is very limited as in the case of palm oil; or at an experimental stage as in the case of kola, cacao, and pepper; or in decline as in the case of rubber. Cattle production, which was almost totally unknown in the Central African Republic until Fulbé (Bororo) pastoralists from Niger and Nigeria moved into the Yadé Plateau in the late 1930s, is still not a major industry. These pastoralists have gradually moved south as far as Zaire and Congo through Haute-Sangha and Basse-Kotto. Their herds may number as many as 650,000 head, but at least 50 percent of the meat eaten in Bangui comes from Chad or Sudan, either by foot or, more rarely, by truck.

Cattle herded by Fulbé pastoralists. Photo courtesy of Thomas O'Toole.

OTHER ECONOMIC ACTIVITIES

Basically there are only three other areas of economic activity that most economists would list as contributing to the gross national product: diamond and gold mining, wood cutting for export, and a number of industries located almost exclusively in Bangui. A very extensive, informal sector of the economy producing goods at a cottage level and providing a large number of services, such as bicycle repair, catering, shoe repair, and petty commerce, has not yet been sufficiently studied or understood. Yet it may well be that this sector plays a more important role in the lives of most Central Africans than does the rest of the economy.

About a dozen forest product companies in Haute-Sangha and the Lobaye produce 24 percent of the country's export revenue. Tropical forests cover 34,000 square kilometers or about 5.5 percent of the Central African Republic, and they represent a large potential resource. Sawmills and plywood production have increased over the years, but during the 1970s the depressed world demand for tropical woods, the difficulties of transport, and the lack of a skilled work force kept production lower than the permitted level

(1 cubic meter per hectare per year on the 95,000 hectares actually scouted for production). In 1980 favorable world market conditions and a deregulation of cutting restrictions under the Kolingba government allowed virtually unrestricted cutting of a variety of valuable trees (sapelli, sipo, ayous, and limba). As a result, existing French, Swiss, Romanian, and Yugoslav firms, some in joint ventures with the government, increased export production to over 177,000 cubic meters in clear-cut operations with no reforestation measures. By mid-1984 the results were already evident. Provisional figures indicated that the total output (logs and sawn timber) was well below the 1980 peak. Exports of 125,000 cubic meters were expected. Flat export prices and persistent transportation difficulties were a partial cause for this decline, but the more crucial reality is that once clear-cutting has been done in tropical forests they do not renew themselves. Thus, the tropical forests of the Central African Republic are becoming a nonrenewable resource already in decline.

Because of the Republic's landlocked position, only mineral products of high value have been exploited. Diamonds represent the main mineral activity, accounting for almost one-third of total exports in 1982. Alluvial diamonds have been extracted for many years from the sandstone areas of Carnot and Mouka-Oudda. The Precambian sandstones of Bangui-Kette have also yielded a considerable supply of diamonds in recent years. Though production and exports have fluctuated as a result of disputes between the government and a succession of external companies, official production was nearly 30,000 carats in 1983. Exports of cut diamonds totaled 3,700 carats in 1982. However, smuggled output is probably even higher.

Producing 23 percent of the official export revenue of the Central African Republic, the diamond industry has an even greater impact on the nation than do forest products. Exploited since 1930, the diamond fields found in a triangle with points at Carnot, Berbérati, and Boda, remain an area of open prospecting. Production remains largely an artisanal affair, with small groups of former farmers working their own pits, sometimes on a seasonal basis.

Diamonds are officially marketed through the *Comptoir National du Diamant* with the major operation being controlled by a New York–based company, Diamond Distributors Incorporated

(DDI). DDI has been active in Central Africa since 1930 and had holdings of over $3 million in the country in the early 1980s. Since 1969 DDI has operated a token national diamond-cutting factory as a joint venture with the Central African government to transform a small percentage of the diamonds exported. Currently DDI has formed a diamond-mining exploration consortium with a French parastatal and the Central African government to control most of the legitimate diamond trade. The Kolingba government's attempt to enforce a 20 percent export tax on diamonds has resulted in a more than 20 percent decline in official production. Diamond smuggling to nearby countries with lower or no export taxes is now more extensive than ever.

At the beginning of the 1970s, the French government started some uranium mining in the Bakouma region. These deposits were estimated to yield as much as 16,000 metric tons of ore with a concentration ratio of approximately 50 percent. The uranium deposits, which in the 1970s were projected to furnish a major source of revenue for the government, have not been exploited further due to excessive initial start-up costs, transportation difficulties, and an insufficient world demand. In addition, the Central African Republic's petroleum potential is currently being assessed by ongoing exploration efforts conducted by the Exxon Corporation.

Between 1952 and 1957, 2 metric tons of gold were extracted from quartz veins north of Nola, and between 1938 and 1951 650 kilograms were extracted from the Roux mine in the West Bangui region. Some gold dust is also found in the Sangha basin, in the Bouar and Baboua areas. In 1979, 69 kilograms of gold were produced, and in 1980, with the aid of foreign mining technicians, production reached an historic high of 521 kilograms. Official gold production fell to 31 kilograms in 1982 with less foreign technical assistance and has not risen much since.

There are few signs of other mineral exploitation starting in the near future. Under Bokassa, Romanian and other East European concerns were active in prospecting for diamonds, gold, and iron. Satellite earth-resource surveys in 1976 suggested that mineral wealth in the country might prove highly promising. Some estimates suggest that as much as 3.5 million metric tons of iron, 300,000 metric tons of copper, and, perhaps some manganese might eventually be mined in the country.

Most Central Africans cannot afford to shop in central Bangui. Photo courtesy of Daniel Gregory.

The hydroelectric plant at Boali on the Mbali River 100 kilometers northwest of Bangui permits the existence of a small-scale industrial sector in the country. With the exception of a peanut-oil plant at Pendé and a textile plant near the falls at Boali, virtually all the industrial output of the country is concentrated in Bangui. Most of these industries are owned by foreign investors and are expected to give quick returns with a minimum of capital investment. The large textile plants controlled by the *Industrie Cotonnière Centrafricaine* that ought to employ 1,200 workers at Bangui and Boali operate at less than capacity because of a shortage of cotton and frequent breakdowns. Often they are closed due to management and upkeep difficulties. A variety of other small industries that are foreign owned and operated continue to function: cigar and cigarette factories, a mattress factory, a coffee-roasting operation, cotton and peanut-oil plants, and a jute bag plant.

Virtually all other industries in Bangui transform imported materials. There is a small bicycle and motorbicycle assembly plant, a Bata shoe factory, a large, prosperous brewery and bottling plant, and two cooking utensil manufacturers that use aluminum imported from Cameroon. Most other enterprises in the capital are scarcely more than single-proprietor workshops and include printers, garage mechanics, brickmakers, carpenters, and the like. In all, about 17,000 employed workers out of a countrywide total of 20,000 work in Bangui. Nationalized retail oil companies at present are functioning in a joint private government company, with day-to-day managerial control maintained by the private sector.

TOURISM

Tourism in the Central African Republic is rooted in the colonial past and the neocolonial present. Rather than drawing on regional strengths and tapping the rather substantial tourist industry that already exists in neighboring Cameroon, the CAR is forced to draw its own clientele from Europe. The colonial administrations and each of the governments since independence have attempted to expand road communications with other countries in the area. Yet transportation between the Central African Republic and Cameroon, better than with any other neighboring country, still remains tenuous. Bangui has far stronger links through air travel and telecommunications with Paris than with Yaoundé. The CAR consequently will be constrained to attract a very high proportion of its tourists directly from France and Europe for the foreseeable future.

Mass tourism of the sort that exists in North Africa, Kenya, Senegambia, and the Seychelles is not likely to become a major source of foreign exchange for the Central African Republic. Those seeking sun, seaside, and cultural exoticism at reasonable prices can find it in more accessible areas of the continent. The CAR's distance from major markets means that it will have to rely on an essentially affluent minority of tourists from Europe, the United States, Japan, and perhaps, Canada, New Zealand, and Australia. These properous, predominantly white few who can afford to travel long distances are attracted by game parks and forests. They want to observe the mythical "uncorrupted traditional societies" that publicity has conjured up as an image of the central part of Africa.

Obviously the Republic has a tremendous potential resource in its wildlife. Located between the major tropical rainforests of Africa and the great open savannas stretching across the continent south of the Sahara, the country has an incomparable variety of wild animals—from forest gorillas to all of the savanna species (elephant, buffalo, giraffe, and antelope) and their natural predators (lion, leopard, and cheetah). In the north of the country ostrich, hippopotamus, and crocodile are common, and even the black rhinoceros is making a comeback.

Travel designed around a program of appreciation of local music, art, crafts, dance, and other such cultural elements in the Central African Republic would be far more difficult. The virtual nonexistence of museums, cultural centers, and traditional festivals in Central Africa means that there is little opportunity for the short-term visitor to enjoy sensitively the few local resources that do exist in the country.

Finally, the Central African Republic's potential for tourism depends not only on its limited tourist attractions and ease of access to European and other affluent tourist markets, but also on its ability to accommodate, cater to, entertain, and transport visitors. In recent years the standards of accommodations have declined, rather than improved. The few hotels and restaurants that do exist suffer from shortages of food, alcoholic beverages, and services. Plumbing and air-conditioning malfunctions, electricity blackouts, petty theft, and water shortages are all to be expected as a matter of course. Furthermore, Bamingui-Bangoran and St. Floris, the major game parks of the country, remain difficult to reach and lack facilities to attract any but the hardiest of tourists. Much better roads and other infrastructure will be necessary before the country is able to receive again the record 8,000 tourists it welcomed in 1978. Even if all the present problems can be overcome, it will be at great cost in foreign exchange, funds that might be spent more profitably in other sectors of the economy. If the Central African Republic is to promote tourism, the major problem will be to ensure that real economic benefits are forthcoming. For example, if most of the supplies needed for the hotels are imported and most of the profits are repatriated by European shareholders, little economic benefit from the tourist industry will accrue to the Central African people. Employment for a few

Central Africans in menial occupations in tourist hotels is hardly a sufficient return for such major investments.

FUTURE PROSPECTS

The present economic outlook for the Central African Republic is not very promising. The country faces growing debt-service problems aggravated by the continued relatively weak position of the French franc in relation to the dollar and the failure of the Central African government to control spending and to trim expenditures on the civil service. The Republic received compensation payments from the EEC through the BEAC for export earning losses in 1982, 1983, and 1984 due to the decline in value of the franc, but this source of foreign exchange for priority imports cannot be repeated indefinitely. France has grown reluctant, and perhaps even unable, to increase its budgetary support for the Kolingba government. Though the Mitterrand government cannot totally relinquish its support because of French investments, strategic minerals, and military bases essential to operations in Chad, France would prefer to secure these interests through a more popular and less extravagant Central African government than the present one.

In terms of recurrent costs and debt-service obligations the Central African Republic has little option, under present conditions, but to return to the harder aid and loan terms of the IMF. Donors hitherto unfamiliar with the country, such as the Netherlands, the Scandinavian countries, and Canada, are unlikely to be attracted by the present regime. France, West Germany, and a few large oil producers currently pledge their aid multiannually and over specific protocol periods. They are likewise unlikely to pledge any additional funds for recurrent costs, and the Central African Republic's economy cannot support any new capital projects. The Republic cannot expect a World Bank structural adjustment loan with an associated IMF standby loan to sustain long-term balance-of-payment support so long as the Kolingba regime is unable to raise government revenue and stimulate production.

Faced with such a thoroughly disturbing economic situation, which can only worsen in the near or distant future if the same methods are employed as in the past, the Republic must adapt a radically different approach to economic development if it is to achieve any significant improvement in the general well-being of its people. This implies a number of breaks with the past, including a rejection by the ruling elite of their obsessive accumulation of imported luxuries. As the Organization of African Unity and the Economic Commission for Africa have pointed out, the people of countries like the Central African Republic can only free themselves from hunger, sickness, ignorance, social and cultural inequalities, and unemployment through self-perpetuating development with the free and effective participation of the entire population.[8] This will necessitate new endogenous development policies to create the material and cultural environment for such change. Under present circumstances, this means a self-reliant agrarian strategy of development for the country as a start. As E. F. Schumacher has argued, development does not start with imported consumer goods; it starts with people and their education, organization, and discipline.[9] The "economistic," technocratic solutions that confuse growth and development, imposed by external agencies and accepted by the bankrupt government of the Central African Republic for want of an alternative, have not worked. A fresh approach that uses scarce resources more wisely will have to be tried because significant new external assistance is not likely to be forthcoming.

NOTES

1. Mahbub ul Haq and S. J. Burki, *Meeting Basic Needs: An Overview* (Washington, D.C.: Poverty and Basic Needs Service, World Bank, 1980).

2. Morris D. Morris, *Measuring the Conditions of the World's Poor: the Physical Quality of Life Index* (New York: Pergamon for the Overseas Development Council, 1979).

3. Claude Ake, *Revolutionary Pressure in Africa* (London: Zed Press Ltd., 1978), 33ff.

4. See for example Samir Amin, *L'accumulation à l'échelle mondiale, critique de la théorie du sous-développement* (Dakar: Institut Fondamental de l'Afrique Noire, 1971).

5. The framework for this analysis of the political economy of the post–World War II Central African Republic draws upon Aguibou Y. Yansane, "Political Economy of Decolonization and Dependency of African States of French Colonial Legacy, 1945–75" in *Decolonization*

and Dependency: Problems of Development of African Societies, ed. Aguibou Y. Yansane (Westport, Conn.: Greenwood Press, 1980), 113–144.

6. OCAM became, in early 1970, the *Organisation Commune Africaine et Mauricienne* when Madagascar withdrew and Mauritius joined.

7. The French Socialists had advocated colonial reform from the mid-1940s and continued to advocate, with Mitterrand at the forefront, far more liberal policies toward the former colonials after independence. For an analysis of French Socialist policies in the 1980s, see Marc Aicardi de Saint Paul, "France's New African Policy," unpublished typescript presented at the Twenty-Fourth Annual Meeting of the African Studies Association, Bloomington, Ind., October 21–24, 1981.

8. See Albert Tevoedjre, "Africa Towards the Year 2000: Final Report on the Joint OAU/ECA Symposium on the Future Development of Africa," *International Foundation for Development Alternatives* (IFDA) Dossier 7 (May 1979).

9. E. F. Schumacher, *Small Is Beautiful* (London: Sphere Books, 1974).

6

The Central African Republic and the World

The foreign policy of a state is normally defined as that set of short- and middle-run objectives vis-à-vis the world polity that are seen as serving the "interests" of the state. Yet even this innocuous definition poses problems when one considers the foreign policy of the Central African Republic. Clearly any discussion of the salient characteristics of Central African foreign policy must begin with an understanding that shifting patterns and outright inconsistencies from both internal and external perspectives make any coherent analysis very difficult.[1]

In general, one can identify two areas of foreign policy activity for the Central African Republic, the global and the African. Neither the global nor the African sphere is completely independent, and within each arena a number of competing interests tend to overlap, interact, and conflict. The CAR's current status dictates that whatever internal economic, political, bureaucratic, military, and ethnic interest groups shape the country's foreign policy, their actions have only a marginal impact on either world or African politics.

Since independence the Central African Republic has been forced to seek assistance from every major political and economic bloc in the world. Yet this has been done in such a haphazard and capricious fashion that no clear pattern emerges. The only possible consistency in Central African diplomacy has been a remarkable willingness to compromise and curry favor with virtually anyone in order to receive aid. Though both the Dacko and the Bokassa regimes paid some lip service to Boganda's idea of a

United States of Latin Africa, little was ever accomplished. Likewise, though each successive regime has sought assistance to build a railroad from Bangui to the Atlantic, none has achieved more than preliminary studies and promises.

Although the Central African Republic is not formally aligned with any bloc of nations, it has generally pursued a pro-Western foreign policy. This seems to have been caused by the state's special relationship with France and the preference of the ruling bureaucratic bourgeoisie for Western affluence rather than by any strong ideological position. Central Africa's leadership has vacillated in its relations with the Muslim world, the two Chinas, and the USSR. It has remained in the Western camp largely out of inertia, need, and personal ties with external funding sources, especially those in France and the United States. The French contribution to the operating budget in 1983 was five billion CFA francs. This increased to ten billion CFA francs in 1984 and rose again in 1985. In 1983 France provided fourteen billion CFA francs in development aid as well and has continued to supply somewhat less development funding since.

FRENCH PRESENCE

The primary foreign policy consideration for the Central African Republic is that, more than twenty-five years after independence, the country is still identified as part of "former French" Africa. The French presence in the CAR has consistently been based on a far more explicit and thus far more visible set of deliberate linkages than the presence of any other powers.

The French penchant for hierarchically structured relationships of command rather than consensus and for imperative rather than cooperative interaction is evident in domestic French social and political institutions. This pattern can also be seen in the structure of "cooperation" between France and the Central African Republic. In the 1960s under President Charles de Gaulle, Jacques Foccart directed French relations with its former colony out of the office of the president as secretary-general for African affairs, in a manner that closely resembled the classic pattern of indirect rule. This state of affairs persisted with even deeper personal and financial involvement under President Valéry Giscard d'Estaing through his chief aide for African affairs, René Journiac, and changed relatively little under the direction of Guy Penne, President François Mitterrand's African affairs expert.

The staffing of a substantial number of senior managerial positions in the Central African government by French nationals has routinized French involvement in the country's political and economic process since independence. Outright military action like that which placed Dacko back in power in 1979 represents only a small, though highly visible, aspect of French influence in the CAR. The French economic and cultural presence, although more discrete, is in the long term far more effective. The past twenty-five years have shown a remarkable continuity in the dependency and relative underdeveloped condition of Central African political and economic structures. This state of affairs seems effectively guaranteed by the country's deteriorating foreign debt situation. The debt-service costs in 1984 were about $25 million, and they rose to about $32.5 million in 1985. Debt servicing required about 17 percent of the country's exports in 1984 and at least 20.5 percent in 1985. Since more than 50 percent of this debt is owed to France, Central African leaders have been forced to remain compliant partners with France in a classic neocolonial situation.

Both Dacko and Bokassa found, to their regret, that they needed to preserve their special relationship with Paris if they wished to remain in power. Even though France has consistently downplayed the economic significance of the Central African Republic and has taken pains to project the image of a policy governed by humanitarian considerations and by a sense of moral obligation, the commercial ties with France are crucial. With 400 to 500 technical assistants and 4,000 other French nationals in residence, to say nothing of the two paratroop companies, one cavalry unit, and one general staff unit of French troops stationed in both Bouar and Bangui, France definitely has a stake in the country.

French interests see Central Africa as a buffer against possible aggression from Libya through Chad into what they perceive as the crucial mining and oil-rich heart of former French Equatorial Africa. It was not an accident that the third Franco-African summit attended by President Giscard d'Estaing was held in Bangui in February 1975. From the French perspective U.S. interests in the

Central African Republic and elsewhere in Africa, limited though they may be in reality, are also viewed in an unfavorable light. To the French, fears of Soviet or Chinese expansionism in Africa are of less consequence than Libyan adventurism or U.S. interference.

THE ROLE OF THE UNITED STATES

From the direct U.S. viewpoint, its foreign policy toward the Central African Republic is of minor significance. Underlying all other considerations, the foreign policy decisions of the United States with respect to the Republic are concerned with the defense of the United States and the "free world." Thus Central Africa is important only insofar as relations with it fit into the U.S. global strategy of defense against communism. Far more interested in Zaire for economic and strategic reasons, the makers of U.S. foreign policy toward the Central African Republic still follow a course of leaving most decisions to the French.

In light of the relatively modest $2.5 million aid programs, including the Peace Corps, that the United States offered the Central African Republic in 1982 (with similar sums in recent years), most U.S. interests are of little consequence to the government of Central Africa. The one notable exception is the Diamond Distributors Incorporated (DDI). (See the discussion of the DDI in Chapter 5.) Because diamonds are the Central African Republic's major export commodity, this single U.S.-based firm cannot be totally ignored by any viable Central African government.

A small number of U.S. missionaries and their dependents along with about seventy Peace Corps volunteers make up the bulk of U.S. citizens residing in the country. Their effect upon political and foreign relations of the country's small ruling elite appears of little consequence.

RUSSIAN AND CHINESE INTERESTS

If other areas of the Central African Republic's foreign policy are unclear, the history of its relationship with the Soviet Union is almost totally opaque. Soviet interests in Central Africa, like those of the United States, are part of the USSR's larger economic and political concerns and often bear little relationship to the dynamics of Central African domestic politics. For the most part, the Soviets show little interest in the CAR beyond their overall policy of capitalizing on any possibilities that give them an ideological or political advantage vis-à-vis the United States. With the exception of some small amount of Eastern bloc economic penetration in the mining and timber industries, the Soviet Union and its allies have played scarcely any role in Central Africa. In August 1964 a high-level Central African mission sent by Dacko called in Moscow as part of a feeble attempt to broaden diplomatic ties with the socialist world. In 1969 Bokassa, in a fit of pique over inadequate deference and subsidies from Paris, suddenly expelled French (and other foreign) technicians and brought diamond mining to a halt. For a short period "scientific socialism" became the order of the day and a top-level diplomatic mission was again dispatched to Moscow in December to explore what financial aid might result from this ideological shift. When this Soviet adventure offered little capital return, Bokassa returned to his Francophile standard. The current Central African government maintains minimal diplomatic relation with the USSR and the Eastern bloc.

The Chinese role in Central African foreign affairs has been more extensive than that of the Soviets. In April 1964 a Chinese delegation from Beijing arrived in Bangui as part of the Zhou Enlai initiative that sought to enhance the Chinese presence in Africa. In August of the same year, Clement Hassen, Dacko's closest adviser, and Ferdinand Bassamongou, the president of the CAR's Economic and Social Council, went to Beijing, seeking aid from the Chinese. Bassamongou announced on August 27 in Beijing that the Central African Republic recognized the People's Republic of China as the only legal representative of the Chinese people. On September 29 commercial as well as technical assistance and cultural exchange agreements between the Central African Republic and the People's Republic of China were signed in Bangui. Dacko underlined his strong support for nonalignment at that time and in November spoke out quite forcibly against the Belgian-American invasion in Stanleyville.

During the entire year of 1965 the Chinese presence in Central Africa was of major importance. A number of Chinese films with themes demonstrating assistance from the People's Republic to the Central African Republic were produced in Sango. A large-scale commercial exposition was planned for December in Bangui and an interest-free, billion-franc CFA loan was given by the Chinese. In November 1965 Dacko was unable to convince the government of China to give the Central Africans this loan in cash in order to bail out his bankrupt government. This failure precipitated Dacko's attempted resignation in December. One of Bokassa's justifications for removing Dacko from power was this flirtation with China. During the Bokassa years the role of the People's Republic remained negligible except for some technical assistance in agriculture.

The current regime, also seeking to find new sources of aid for virtual bankruptcy has again turned to the People's Republic for help. Following a presidential visit to China July 4–8, 1983, General Kolingba obtained a 5.5 billion CFA franc, interest-free loan from Beijing to finance agricultural and infrastructure projects. The terms of this loan are very liberal; there is a ten-year grace period. In this case the capital goods component of the loan is specifically committed to the financing of new radio transmitters and a new hospital for Bangui, projects for which the Chinese will deliver both the technological assistance and materials. For the People's Republic, aid to the CAR is no longer simply an ideological or propaganda statement but rather a calculated investment in further sales of materials and know-how on the African continent.

ISRAEL

Like many African nations in the early 1960s, the Central African Republic established relations with Israel. Economic considerations were the major factor spurring Central Africa to strengthen its ties with this small country because Israel was willing to share its technical expertise on relatively reasonable terms in order to pave the way for the penetration of Central African markets for Israel's light industrial goods. Official relations between the Republic and Israel date from Dacko's state visit to Israel in June 1962. During 1964 and 1965 Israel granted Central Africa a number of loans and created the *Comptoir Israëlo-Cen-*

trafricain (CIC) to direct a series of agricultural research institutes. Several youth camps, the *Jeunesse Pionnière Nationale* (JPN), were also founded in villages and placed under the direction of Israeli officers in a vain attempt to create centers on the lines of kibbutzim.

Of far more importance during Dacko's first administration was the Israeli role in the diamond industry. In late 1961 Dacko granted a purchasing monopoly to a joint stock company formed by Israelis and Central Africans and allowed it full exemption from export duties. Though this lucrative arrangement for the Israelis was restricted at the end of 1963, the Israelis, during Dacko's second brief period in power, once more became and remain today one of the Central African Republic's principal diamond traders.

Bokassa's able minister of national economy, Captain Timothée Malendoma, set up the *Office National du Diamant* on June 20, 1966, which worked effectively with the Israelis and an international consortium through 1968 to regularize the diamond industry in Central Africa. Unfortunately, Bokassa's greed almost destroyed this working relationship when he expelled the foreign technicians in late 1969. The Israeli ambassador was withdrawn in May 1970 because of this dispute over diamond mining, but the Israeli diamond-buying firm, *Centrafricain Pituach,* was back in operation by September 1970. Relations between the Israelis and the mercurial Bokassa were never stable. In October 1973 Bokassa broke off diplomatic relations with Israel in support of the United Arab Republic.

Relations with Israel were not a major issue during the second Dacko government. Colonel Kolingba's finance minister visited Jerusalem and Tel Aviv in July 1983 and was received by the Israeli prime minister. Formal relations were not reestablished at that time, but the military support and diamond marketing and mining expertise that Israel can supply the Central African Republic are so important that it is likely that renewed relations with Israel will continue to grow in importance for a long time to come.

FRANCOPHONE AFRICAN RELATIONS

Boganda's final attempts in late 1958 and early 1959 failed to create a federation of the four states of French Equatorial Africa, but a series of conferences during 1963, 1964, and 1965 established the *Union Douanière et Economique de l'Afrique Centrale* (UDEAC), including Cameroon, Central African Republic, Chad, Congo, and Gabon. This customs union seeks to harmonize planning, industrial development, telecommunications, and fiscal and social policies. In 1975, the UDEAC states formed the Central African States Development Bank and in January 1985 Equatorial Guinea joined the CFA franc zone through its membership in this bank.

Dacko always sought to maintain relatively good relations with neighboring French-speaking states. In the March 1981 election Dacko's party received at least some support from Gabon, Cameroon, and Zaire. Furthermore, the Central African Republic, unlike its immediate Francophone neighbors, continues to participate in the *Organisation Commune Africaine et Mauricienne* (OCAM) because the organization's headquarters are in Bangui. Most of the political functions of OCAM have been replaced by annual Franco-African summits, which the Central African Republic, Chad, and Gabon never fail to attend and Cameroon has avoided.

Upon his accession to power, Bokassa sought immediate diplomatic representation from the original UDEAC nations. He even mentioned closer ties with Congo-Kinshasa on a visit there in mid-1966. His brief excursion in 1968 into a more limited *Union des Etats de l'Afrique Centrale* (UEAC) was short-lived. By December 10, 1968, Bokassa had suspended relations with Congo-Kinshasa and rejoined UDEAC. The off-and-on nature of Central African relations with Mobutu's government persisted throughout most of the Bokassa regime, but by 1977 the two dictators had achieved a mutually supportive stance, with both citing common kinship ties among the peoples of the Ubangi River. There is good reason to believe that at least 100 Zairian paratroopers assisted Bokassa in crushing the student revolts of 1979. President Mobutu visited Bangui from June 15 to 17, 1980, and signed a cooperative agreement for the construction of a dam at Mobayo, 450 kilometers east of Bangui. This cooperative project with Zaire, planned in the second Dacko administration to provide electricity for the Basse-Kotto and Mbomou regions as well as portions of north-central Zaire, was never realized.

The Kolingba government has continued generally cooperative relations with Zaire. At a summit meeting in Libreville on October

17, 1983, Kolingba, along with the heads of state of Gabon, Cameroon, Chad, Congo, Equatorial Guinea, São Tomé and Príncipe, Zaire, Rwanda, and Burundi signed a treaty formally constituting the Economic Community of Central African States (ECOCAS). In December 1983 Kolingba presided over the seventeenth summit of UDEAC states, held in Bangui. This conference also saw the admission of Equatorial Guinea into the union. Though far from fulfilling Boganda's grandiose dreams of a United States of Latin Africa, the Central African Republic continues to play a modest role in Francophone African politics.

LIBYA AND CHAD

Documentation of Libyan intervention in Central African affairs since Colonel Muammar Qaddafy took over the government of Libya in 1969 is virtually impossible. Most of the evidence is circumstantial and quite inconsistent. The first certain event was Qaddafy's official state visit to Bangui on October 17, 1976. When Bokassa announced his conversion to Islam and took the name Salah Eddine Ahmed Bou-Kassa three days later, it appeared that a slight pro-Islamic stance, begun with Bokassa's visit to the United Arab Republic in April 1970, might actually be coming to fruition. Bokassa also had signed a twenty-year friendship treaty with Iraq in early 1972. Bokassa was in Tripoli seeking support from Qaddafy for his regime on September 21, 1979, when the French returned Dacko to power.

In January 1980 the Dacko government broke relations with Libya, accusing it of interfering in the internal affairs of the Central African Republic. The success of Libyan forces in establishing themselves in Chad in late 1980 made Dacko and his French backers even more upset. On December 19, 1980, Bokassa was brought to trial in absentia on a number of charges including plotting against the security of the state by signing a secret defense pact with Libya. When Qaddafy announced plans for a union of Libya and Chad at the beginning of 1981, Dacko and the French felt clearly threatened. In the March 1981 presidential campaign Dacko used Ange Patassé's connections with Libya as a major issue against him. Yet within a little more than a year after achieving power on September 1, 1981, General Kolingba had signed cooperative agreements with Libya to hasten the exploitation of Central Africa's mineral resources. A joint committee for economic and social cooperation was also set up at the end of 1982. The CAR reportedly received 500 million French francs in Libyan aid at that time, and assistance was also forthcoming in the training of Central African personnel for a new armored division. At least fifty Libyan army instructors were present in Central Africa for the next six months. Although Kolingba hotly denied it, the CAR's closest neighbors accused the Libyans of being in Central Africa to destabilize the anti-Libyan Hissène Habré regime in southern Chad.

Under French pressure Kolingba sent the Libyan instructors home in May 1983 and moved pro-Libyan Lieutenant Colonel Jean-Louis Gervil Yambala from the Foreign Ministry to the less sensitive Department of Trade and Industry. In April 1983 Yambala had accompanied Kolingba on a visit to Tripoli where, according to Libya, the Central African leader had sought to "familiarize himself with Libya's pioneering democratic experiment." To what extent Kolingba's flirtation with Libya was simply a ploy to pressure the Mitterrand government into granting Central Africa more aid is unclear. As long as French intervention in Chad is a major part of that nation's foreign policy, the potential for Libyan intervention in the affairs of the Central African Republic remains real.

TIES WITH OTHER AFRICAN NATIONS

The only other African country of major importance to the Central African Republic's foreign policy has been the Republic of South Africa. As with most international relations of the CAR, the relationship with the Republic of South Africa is based upon Central Africa's continued search for additional aid and revenue. Linkages with South Africa are a good example of the Central African Republic's often incoherent international relations history. In February and March 1975 two Central African ministerial delegations were invited, through French intermediaries, to visit Johannesburg. In announcing the second of these missions, the Central African minister of state for foreign affairs declared candidly that, although Central Africa was opposed to apartheid, his country was in no position to turn down any possibilities of aid.

Later in the year the Republic of South Africa sent a large delegation to Bangui to examine suitable projects for South African assistance. No precise official agreement was ever published, but a figure of over $250 million to be granted over the following ten years was widely reported. This aid included a four-million-rand loan granted in February 1975 to construct a 500-room tourist hotel, construction of which, under the direct supervision of white South Africans, continued into the first year of Dacko's second administration. A second loan of six million rand resulted in the construction of more than two dozen prefabricated houses in Bangui. Poorly designed and requiring constant air-conditioning, these units nonetheless were considered prestigious residences in the late 1970s for middle-level Central African bureaucrats and some expatriate teachers and technicians. The two governments were also thought to have agreed on a feasibility study for a railroad linking Bangui to the Atlantic, a project for which the Central African Republic has consistently sought support. Cooperation was also thought to have been considered in the marketing and mining of Central Africa's diamonds and, probably, uranium. A projected visit by Bokassa to the Republic of South Africa never occurred, and under Dacko the linkages with South Africa gradually declined. Kolingba has made only tentative gestures toward renewing these ties.

Central African diplomatic ties with Anglophone Africa have been relatively unimportant. In January 1964 Dacko received a Ghanaian mission that proposed that Bangui ought to become the capital of a united Africa. Dacko did not attend the Pan African Conference in Ouagadougou on March 10, 1965, but he did announce his acceptance of the Ghanaian idea of a continental government just before leaving for the Addis Ababa conference on May 20, 1965. With Bokassa in power and Kwame Nkrumah deposed in February 1966, this great dream of pan-African union ceased to have any viability.

Bokassa made a state visit in late 1966 to the Sudan where he agreed to a draft plan to extend the railroad from Port Sudan to within the Central African Republic. This excursion into diplomatic linkages with the only former British colonial territory sharing a border with Central Africa was short lived. Caught up in a series of endless bloody attacks and retaliations between the sophisticated Muslim-dominated northern government forces and the often oppressed Christian and animist southern resisters, the Sudanese had little surplus to devote to constructing noneconomic railroads. At best they hoped simply to have assurance that the Central African Republic would not aid the armed southerners who often sought haven among the other refugees from the Sudan streaming into Central Africa and neighboring countries. Colonel Jaafar al-Nimiery's bloodless coup on May 25, 1969, led to a reduction in the fighting and consequently the Sudan's need to maintain relations with the Bokassa regime.

After a visit to Uganda in August 1972, Bokassa expressed his admiration for Idi Amin's expulsion of the Asian minority and established close diplomatic ties with the Amin government. In December 1976 Amin was one of the first to congratulate Bokassa on his self-proclamation as emperor. Nothing concrete ever came of this mutual admiration between these two flamboyant and arbitrary former colonial military officers. Within six months of the overthrow of Amin in April 1979, his fellow tyrant, Bokassa, had been deposed through French intervention. Nothing remained of their personalistic diplomatic overtures.

AT THE UNITED NATIONS AND ELSEWHERE

The Central African Republic has been a member of the United Nations and its specialized agencies since 1960. Beyond a general adherence to a rather bland pan-Africanism and a token support for the principle of nonalignment common to most independent African states, the Central African Republic has made little impact at the United Nations. As a member of the Organization of African Unity (OAU), the Central African Republic rhetorically shares a common commitment to anticolonialism and racism with other African states. The Central African Republic has occasionally joined in the call for reform of the international economy as a means of combating Third World poverty and aiding economic development. At the UN headquarters in New York, the Central African mission is hardly noticed. Its delegates are often absent from the sessions, and when they are present their role has never been one of leadership. The relationships the Republic has established with non-African states have, with relatively few exceptions, been compatible with its ongoing special relationship with France.

Close links to France have never allowed Central Africans to play a major role in the United Nations Commission for Trade and Development. The UN Development Program (UNDP) mission to the Central African Republic has often operated in a paternalistic fashion; its non-African technicians and experts guide about $18 million a year in aid and develop projects with little reference to Central African inputs. With the often chaotic state of Central African administration and the lack of clear direction and planning, this is probably inevitable but certainly places the CAR in a disadvantageous position from which to attempt to affect UN support for its own development needs.

The aid donors' conference convened in October 1984 in Bangui was cohosted by the local UNDP office with the passive participation of the Central African government. Conferences of this sort are designed to stimulate traditional donors to pledge more and to attract donors who have not previously shown any interest in the country. Like the one held in Bangui in the spring of 1980, this meeting had little long-term effect on the nation's budgetary impasse. It only reinforced the nation's dependency on the United Nations and other funders for assistance. After the 1980 conference the IMF stepped in to grant a small standby credit each year. After the 1984 conference the World Bank agreed to intercede and placed foreign experts in the administration to assist in external debt payment, budgetary, and parastatal management under an $8.5 million technical assistance project. Kolingba has only halfheartedly and reluctantly assented to the austerity measures imposed by the intervention of these agencies, and very little improvement has resulted.

NOTES

1. No comprehensive political study of the Central African Republic has emerged since that by Pierre Kalck, *Histoire de la Rėpublique Centrafricaine* (Paris: Editions Berger-Levrault, 1974), though for the

period covered this is an informed and judicious account. For events after 1974 this chapter relies upon such sources as the *African Contemporary Record; Revue Française d'études politiques Africaines, Quarterly Economic Review of Gabon, Congo, Cameroon, Central African Republic, Chad, Equatorial Guinea; Africa News; Afrique-Asia;* and *Jeune Afrique.*

7

Central Africa and the Future

The Central African Republic has been pillaged for centuries and, in the opinion of many, the process is still going on. The results are obvious to even the casual observer. The country is underdeveloped, fragmented, and poverty stricken. Even those people, inside and outside the CAR, who most wish it the best possible future are far from optimistic. Despite the fact that the country has important mineral deposits and could export significant amounts of cotton, coffee, timber, and textiles, precious little of the wealth that is and could be generated ever seeps down to the population at large. What is not expropriated by foreign interests the small bureaucratic bourgeoisie fritters away on conspicuous consumption and nonproductive investment. It is unlikely that the current military rule in the Central African Republic will generate the kind of enlightened and dedicated government that might make the country, if not prosperous, at least less blatantly dependent and poor.

MILITARY RULE: HOW LONG?

Most of the Western scholarship about army coups in Africa, especially Francophone Africa, gives too little insight into the personal motives of ambitious officers. Maintaining, as many scholars do, that military takeovers in Africa are the result of government inefficiency, corruption, ethnic cleavages, and intraelite strife, as Samuel Decalo has pointed out, is virtually tautological.[1] It is obvious that leadership in the Central African Republic in

1965 was afflicted with nepotism, vacillation, and corruption. Yet the most important "cause" of the country's first military coup was the personal ambition of Colonel Bokassa, not the persisting budgetary crisis or the rampant corruption. The most widespread complaint of junior officers and the rank and file at the time was not so much government corruption (though again, this was one of the official reasons for the coup) as the unequal competition from politicians who were able, among other things, to acquire the best mistresses in Bangui.[2] Likewise, though General Kolingba justified the coup of September 1, 1981, on the grounds that the second Dacko administration had violated the constitution and was incapable of solving the nation's economic crisis, Kolingba's promises to restore civilian rule when he had set the country right dissolved as opportunities for official junkets and spoils presented themselves.

It is clear that the military regimes of Bokassa and Kolingba have not been more successful than the two Dacko civilian regimes that they replaced. Once in charge, the Central African military has not proven to be the advanced, Westernized, well-disciplined, "detribalized," and technically oriented institution that organization theorists in the 1960s had suggested military rule in Africa might prove to be. Neither Bokassa nor Kolingba, in assuming control of the state, had much success in reducing corruption, in avoiding the bickering and politicking of different factions, and in overcoming ethnic rivalries. And neither regime proved able to address itself more directly and efficiently than the civilian governments to the problems of poor administration, lack of economic and social development, and continued neocolonial dependency.

Kolingba's military regime possesses no greater potential for assisting development than the larger society from which it is drawn. It demonstrates few of the qualities once held to be inherent within modern military structures: chain of command, bureaucratic organization, well-defined areas of responsibility, technological expertise, and basic literacy. In fact the Central African army is, like many African armies, "a coterie of distinct armed camps owing primary clientelist allegiance to a handful of mutually competitive officers of different ranks seething with a variety of corporate, ethnic, and personal grievances."[3] The Kolingba regime is subject to all the strains, tensions, rivalries, abuses, and weaknesses of the civilian government it replaced.

Based as it is on two very divergent sociopolitical structures, the Kolingba regime is incapable of forming the organic, highly integrated relationship between the government and the majority of the population that is necessary to provide viable alternatives to current patterns. In one view, the Kolingba regime is little more than an extension of the unitary political and military structure imposed on Central Africa by the French. Consequently for most of the people the Kolingba government is not an integral part of Central African society, but an apolitical, asocial structure whose purpose is to serve itself and its French supporters. In another view, that of a smaller number of Kolingba's own Yakoma ethnic group, the government simply represents the normal and natural persistence of social and political patterns that evolved in conjunction with predatory trading diaspora since the early seventeenth century.[4] As long as Kolingba is able to distribute spoils widely among his own lineages and clients, as his trading ancestors would have done, he will hold their support. Unfortunately for him, the spoils are few, his followers no longer share them with their respective corporate groups as tradition once dictated, and the rest of the nation, whether seeing Kolingba as simply another *mboundjou-voko* (Sango term for white black) out to exploit them or as a traditional African ruler from a historical enemy group, has little reason for allegiance to him or his government. Kolingba will last only so long as the French government finds him less embarrassing than would be the negative impact caused by their intervention to establish another government.

DILEMMAS OF STATE BUILDING

There is little sign that personal rule in the Central African Republic will soon give way to more institutionalized forms of conducting the affairs of state. To date none of the rulers has actually succeeded in institutionalizing the administration of state business. Widespread ethnic nepotism, to which each leader has ultimately resorted, has almost completely undermined the colonial centralized-bureaucratic organ inherited from France. Bureaucratization as a vehicle for state building has not succeeded in the

Central African Republic; instead, there has been a continual deterioration in the reliability and capabilities of state organizations. The decline in staff competence has reduced administrative effectiveness. Administrative responsibility has virtually disappeared as officials forsake objective choices of personal whim and the satisfaction of kinship and descent group demands.

Short-lived solutions to the problems of administrative incompetence and nepotism have been achieved by the Central African Republic rulers only when they have been able to identify projects as crucial to their own interests. By making a conspicuous display of their concern for these specific projects they have been able, for a time, to make the officials responsible for carrying them out think long and hard before sabotaging them. The brief but rather impressive success of "Operation Bokassa" in increasing cotton production is a case in point. Although ultimately based on false premises about both world market conditions and local agricultural practices and undermined by Bokassa's own profit taking, this program demonstrated the importance of a ruler's personal preoccupation in achieving specific short-run goals. Unfortunately no consistent pattern of promoting economic or other policy goals has emerged and been pursued for more than a year or two.

The only really consistent dimension of state building to emerge in the Central African Republic to date has been the attempt by each of the country's three rulers to establish an unrestricted presidential office for himself. Whether through the writing of new constitutions, elections, or installing himself as "emperor," each of the country's rulers has resorted to some legitimizing device for his personal rule after seizing power. To date none of them, when pushed to the limit, has shown respect for the office he has created and the rules he has defined. Rather, when their own interests have been threatened, all three of them have arbitrarily altered the areas of jurisdiction, rights and powers, and tenure in office in order to remain in control. The institution of the presidency and other high state offices has grown progressively weaker with each new regime.

Kolingba faces little pressure for the restoration of open government because constitutional government has never really existed in the Central African Republic. Constitutional transfer of power and succession have no precedent in the CAR. What political order does exist rests on personal arrangements subject to arbitrary repudiation. Politics is "palace politics" involving members of the dominant ruling "clan" with limited participation by a wider circle of bureaucratic bourgeoisie who themselves represent only a small segment of the country's diverse social groups.

It is clear that none of the leaders in the Republic has had much success in building an efficient, nationally oriented, and stable administration. Neither Western liberal conceptions of parliamentary democracy nor any traditional African consensus forms of rule have evolved. An all too common progression of one party, to "no party" and, finally military coup has occurred in the Central African Republic. And, as elsewhere on the continent, the corruption of politicians and the decline of public morality figure prominently in Central African politics.

SOME POSSIBLE SCENARIOS

Based on the experience of the Central African Republic and other African nations, and a historical evaluation of nation-states throughout the world, one of three basic types of political systems might be expected to evolve from the inherently unstable regimes that have existed thus far. In one scenario, the civil service, the technocrats, the liberal professionals, the educators, and the small African business class might succeed in establishing a relatively efficient and benevolent bureaucratic oligarchy like that in Senegal or the Ivory Coast. A second possibility is that a highly articulate, ideologically sophisticated vanguard might promote a movement based on the participation of the urban and rural poor and begin the transition to participatory socialism, along the lines that the leadership in Mozambique claims to be following. A third scenario is that the present leadership, or another much like it, will consolidate its personal rule[5] until toppled by a plot or coup or until death intervenes. A corollary to this third scenario seems quite plausible. Members of the current regime or another similar one could gradually come to accept a more reasonable level of profit from their positions, thereby allowing a more or less stable equilibrium to be achieved among local power groups within the present neocolonial situation.

The likelihood of a Central African bourgeoisie that sees the state as more than an instrument for its own accumulation of wealth achieving power and actually beginning to develop a self-reliant national economy is remote. In the first place, there are still far too few educated people outside the government administration. Few wealthy planters, traders, small businessmen, and salaried employees exist, and the educational establishment is virtually an arm of the government bureaucracy. The handful of progressive intellectuals, labor leaders, and professionals who support Abel Goumba and his FPO represent an insignificant minority among a relatively small urban population in this overwhelming rural society. Even if Goumba and his followers were able to gain control of the central administration, there is little objective evidence in his followers' personal histories or public statements to suppose that this weak indigenous bourgeoisie would be able to do much more than renegotiate the terms of dependency for the Central African Republic, in spite of Goumba's own deep personal commitment to reform. The rural poor and the marginalized populations of Bangui and the few regional towns have never actually participated in the formation of policy. However, the basic concepts of impersonality necessary for efficient public administration are at odds with the pervasive clientelism that has been the only hope, historically, of the poor in the Central African Republic. This incongruence remains a roadblock to progressive reform.[6]

To date the former leaders of the MLPC and the MCLN, Ange Patassé and Rodolphe Iddi Lala, even more than Goumba have stressed their connections with the aspirations of the masses and their championship of the struggles of the poor. Calling for armed revolt against first the Dacko and later the Kolingba regime, these two leaders have not presented programs of ideological clarity or even coherence. If outside supporters came to the aid of either of these two leaders alone or even in a coalition with Goumba and helped him to power, the chances are that promises of participatory socialism would be betrayed. Even if these leaders themselves were heavily indoctrinated with elements of socialism, most of their immediate following is clearly petite bourgeoisie. Faced with the very real problems of mobilizing and radicalizing the rural poor and the marginalized urban populations, of disengaging from the exploitative relationships with Western companies and individuals, and of revitalizing productive forces, these leaders might easily be overwhelmed by frustration and a sense of impotence. Preoccupied with bare survival and unable to do much to advance socialism, leaders like Iddi Lala and, quite probably, Ange Patassé, even if restrained by Goumba, would seek release in some forms of symbolic success. It is all too easy to look for scapegoats, and the enemies of such revolutions are found everywhere. The rhetoric of violence, already loosened by Iddi Lala and Patassé, could easily disintegrate into the sort of quasi-class violence that journalists writing about Africa often call "tribalism."

The most likely scenario is that the present government, or its successors in the near future, will move beyond mere clientelism to tyranny[7] as public funds and French subsidies prove insufficient to satisfy the wants and needs of their ethnic and kindred supporters. With few major industries to tax, little alien-owned business to indigenize, and virtually no surplus to extract from the overwhelmingly subsistence-based economy, the presidential patronage necessary to maintain a regime in power is not present within the existing socioeconomic system. In the worst possible case, Kolingba or a successor would be so driven by fear and the desire to remain in power that he would create an increasingly abusive regime like that of the late Francisco Macias Nguema Biyogo of Equatorial Guinea, the deposed Idi Amin Dada of Uganda, or the former emperor Jean-Bedel Bokassa.

Another less brutal alternative within the present socioeconomic system is that Kolingba or his successors would be able to negotiate agreements with multinationals and/or a variety of governments that would generate enough economic growth to allow a ruling oligarchy to extract a sufficient share of the wealth to keep the country quiescent. This neocolonial alternative[8] is premised upon a continued increase in productivity in the cotton sector, rehabilitation of the Bangui textile mills, reduction of smuggling in the diamond sector, revival of gold production, and the possibility that promised uranium and oil reserves might actually be tapped. Such a neocolonial system might continue to succeed for the next twenty-five years because even if an articulate "labor aristocracy" in Bangui and a few of the larger regional towns begins to emerge, it will not become so large that it will not be able to be bought off with the small surplus that can be extracted from the more numerous but largely inarticulate rural poor. These inequities may work against political stability in the very long run but in the short run may actually be the most viable alternatives to absolute tyranny.

It may well be that the only real possibilities for economic and social development as well as political stability in the Central African Republic will depend upon the evolution of new social and political structures. The present military regime is apparently incapable of initiating the long process required to bring about a different, less alienating, more peaceful, and productive Central African Republic through participatory development.[9] Whatever social, political, economic, technological, or ideological solutions emerge in response to the Central African Republic's very real problems, it is unlikely that viable alternatives will emerge from the present leadership.

In the meantime it should not be forgotten that most Central Africans never have been totally integrated into monetarized market circuits subject to state control or into a national political system. Hence their failure to participate in the political process or to comply with government economic directives often reflects their nonengagement and unwillingness to enter into an economic and political arena on unfavorable terms rather than a lack of economic and political motivation. Just as the various Central African governments have rarely been able to tap more than a tiny percentage of the country's crop-producing potential so too have they been unable to engage the loyalties of a large percentage of the population. Most Central Africans consume or store the bulk of their own production rather than selling it, and most Central Africans find little value in adherence to a remote state that has little direct influence, positive or negative, on their lives. The political and economic realities of many people in the area arbitrarily defined by mapmakers as the Central African Republic have little to do with the equally arbitrary apparatus of the state or the political and bureaucratic bourgeoisie that dominates it.

Perhaps the day may come when the as yet unheard from majority of Central Africans will play a role in building a more viable nation. Such progress is possible but, based upon the present situation, it should by no means be seen as absolutely so ordained by history. Historically centralized states are the exception rather than the rule in much of Africa, and it may be that the Central African Republic is little more than externally imposed fiction with minimal future in its present form.

NOTES

1. See Samuel Decalo, *Coups and Army Rule in Africa: Studies in Military Style* (New Haven: Yale University Press, 1976), 5–37.

2. J. M. Lee, *African Armies and Civil Order* (New York: Praeger, 1969), 100.

3. Decalo, *Coups and Army Rule in Africa,* 14–15.

4. See the discussion of this phenomenon in regard to Bokassa in Thomas E. O'Toole, "Jean-Bedel Bokassa: Neo-Napoleon or Traditional African Ruler?" In *The Cult of Power: Dictators in the Twentieth Century,* ed. Joseph Held (New York: Columbia University Press, 1983), 95–106.

5. See Robert H. Jackson and Carl G. Rosberg, *Personal Rule in Black Africa* (Berkeley: University of California Press, 1982) for an explanation of this term.

6. On the concept of clientelism see Richard Sandbrook, *The Politics of Basic Needs: Urban Aspects of Assaulting Poverty in Africa* (Toronto: University of Toronto Press, 1982), 195–198.

7. On the concept of the tyrant see Jackson and Rosberg, *Personal Rule in Black Africa,* 234–265.

8. Sandbrook, *The Politics of Basic Needs,* 83–90.

9. Guy Gran, *Development by People* (New York: Praeger, 1983). This work outlines the general theory of participatory development; a preliminary outline for putting into operation this alternative for the Central African Republic can be drawn from Guy Gran, "From the Official Future to a Participatory Future: Rethinking Development Policy and Practice in Rural Zambia," *Africa Today* 30 (1983, published March 15, 1984), 5–22.

Selected Bibliography

GENERAL WORKS

Biarnes, Pierre. *L'Afrique aux Africains: 20 ans d'indépendence en Afrique noire francophone.* Paris: Armand Colin, 1980.

Bourget, Marie. *Merveilleux pays: République Centrafricaine.* Versailles: Delroisse, 1968.

Denis, Vennetier and Wilmet. *L'Afrique centrale et orientale.* Paris: Presses Universitaires de France, 1971.

Grellet, Gérard, Monique Mainguet, and Pierre Soumille. *La République Centrafricaine.* Presses Universitaires de France, 1982.

Kalck, Pierre. *Réalités Oubanguiennes.* Paris: Editions Berger-Levrault, 1959.

______. *Central African Republic: A Failure in Decolonization,* translated by Barbara Thomson. New York: Praeger, 1971.

______. *Histoire de la République Centrafricaine.* Paris: Editions Berger-Levrault, 1974.

______. *Historical Dictionary of the Central African Republic,* translated by Thomas O'Toole. Metuchen, N.J.: Scarecrow Press, 1980.

Lamb, David. *The Africans.* New York: Random House, 1982.

Zoctizoum, Yarisse. *Histoire de la Centrafrique,* 2 vols. Paris: L'Harmattan, 1983.

HISTORY

Austen, Ralph A., and Rita Headrick. "Equatorial Africa Under Colonial Rule." In *History of Central Africa,* Vol. 2, edited by David Birmingham and Phyllis M. Martin. London: Longman, 1983.

Banville, Ghislain de. *Ouaka 1900–1920.* Bambari, CAR: Centre Culturel Saint-Jean, 1983.

Bayle des Hermens, Roger de. *Recherches prehistoriques en République Centrafricaine*. Paris: Editions Labethno, 1973.

Ballard, John A. "Four Equatorial States." In *National Unity and Regionalism in Eight African States*, edited by Gwendolen M. Carter. Ithaca, N.Y.: Cornell University Press, 1966.

Chafford, George. *Les carnets sécrets de la décolonisation*. Paris: Berger-Levrault, 1967.

Coquery-Vidrovitch, Catherine. *Le Congo au temps des grandes compagnies concessionnaires, 1898–1930*. Paris: La Haye, 1972.

Cordell, Dennis D. *Dar al-Kuti and the Last Years of the Trans-Saharan Slave-Trade*. Madison: University of Wisconsin Press, 1984.

______. "The Savanna Belt of North-Central Africa." In *History of Central Africa*, Vol. 1, edited by David Birmingham and Phyllis M. Martin. London: Longman, 1983.

Dampierre, Eric de. *Un Ancien royaume bandia du Haut-Oubangui*. Paris: Plon, 1967.

Harms, Robert W. *River of Wealth, River of Sorrow: The Central Zaire Basin in the Era of the Slave and Ivory Trade, 1500–1891*. New Haven: Yale University Press, 1981.

Kalck, Pierre. "Barthélemy Boganda, Tribun et visionnaire de l'Afrique Centrale." In *Les Africains*, Vol. 3, edited by Charles-André Julien et al. Paris: Editions Jeune Afrique, 1977.

Makouta-Mboukou, Jean-Pierre. *Les Français en Afrique noire*. Paris: Bordas, 1973.

Nzabakomada-Yakoma, Raphael. "Karnou, Prophète de l'indépendence en Afrique Centrale." In *Les Africains*, Vol. 4, edited by Charles-André Julien, et al. Paris: Editions Jeune Afrique, 1977.

O'Toole, Thomas. "The 1929–1931 Gbaya Insurrection in Ubangui-Shari: Messianic Movement or Village Self Defense?" *Canadian Journal of African Studies* 18 (1984), 329–344.

Serre, Jacques. *Histoire de la République Centrafricaine (1890–1960)*. Bangui: Ecole Nationale d'Administration, 1964.

Suret-Canale, Jean. *French Colonialism in Tropical Africa 1900–1945*, translated by Till Gottheimer. New York: Universe Books, 1971.

Teulières, André. "Oubangui et France Libre," *Revue française d'études politiques Africaines* 117 (Sept. 1975), 55–72.

Thompson, Virginia, and Richard Adloff. *The Emerging States of French Equatorial Africa*. Stanford, Calif.: Stanford University Press, 1960.

Vidal, Pierre. *La Civilisation mégalithique de Bouar: Prospections et fouilles, 1962–1966*. Paris: Editions Labethno, 1969.

Weinstein, Brian. *Eboué*. New York: Oxford University Press, 1977.

Young, Crawford, "The Northern Republics 1960–1980." In *History of Central Africa,* Vol. 2, edited by David Birmingham and Phyllis M. Martin. London: Longman, 1983.

POLITICS AND GOVERNMENT

Ammi-Oz, Moshe. "Le Prononciamento du chef d'état Centrafricain." *Revue française d'études politiques Africaines* 149 (1978):45–61.

Dreux Breze, Joachim de. *Le Problème du regroupement en Afrique equatoriale.* Paris: Librairie Générale de Droit et de Jurisprudence, 1968.

Gueret, François. *La Formation de l'unité nationale en République Centrafricaine.* Paris: Faculté de Droit et des Sciences Politiques, University of Paris, 1970, typescript.

Iddi Lala, Rodolphe. "Contribution à l'étude de l'évolution socio-politique en République Centrafricaine." Thesis, University of Paris, 1971.

Kalck, Pierre. *La République Centrafricaine.* Paris: Editions Berger-Levrault, 1971.

O'Toole, Thomas E. "Jean-Bedel Bokassa: Neo-Napoleon or Traditional African Ruler?" In *The Cult of Power: Dictators in the Twentieth Century,* edited by Joseph Held. New York: Columbia University Press, 1983.

Pean, Pierre. *Bokassa Ier.* Paris: Alain Moreau, 1977.

Rougeaux, Jean-Pierre. "Le Partie unique en République Centrafricaine: Le MESAN." Paris: Faculté de Droit et des Sciences Politiques, University of Paris, 1968, mimeo.

Serre, Jacques. "Six ans de gouvernement Dacko (1960–1966)." *Revue française d'études politiques africaines* (Paris) 117 (1975):73–104.

Thiam, Doudou. *The Foreign Policy of African States.* New York: Praeger, 1965.

White, Dorothy S. *Black Africa and De Gaulle: From the French Empire to Independence.* University Park, Pa.: Pennsylvania State University Press, 1979.

Zanga, Antoine. "Quinze ans de déstabilisation en Centrafrique. De l'action humanitaire au dangereux précédent." *Le Monde Diplomatique* (April 1980).

THE ECONOMY

Dumont, René. *Le Difficile développement agricole de la République Centrafricaine.* Paris: Annales de l'Institut National Agronomique (IV), 1966.

Goumba, Abel. *Analyse des conditions préparatoires à la purification sanitaire en République Centrafricaine.* Paris: private printing, 1972.

Hugot, Pierre. "République Centrafricaine: Du plan intérimaire au plan quadriennal." *Industries et travaux d'outre-mer,* Paris (January 1966):21–27.

Kalck, Pierre. "Les Possibilités du développement économique et social de l'Oubangui-Chari." Doctoral thesis, University of Paris, 1958.

______. "Un Pays trop peu connu: La République Centrafricaine." *Forum Geneva* (GATT) (March 1965):7–9.

Maidou, Henri et al. *Philosophie de l'opération Bokassa,* 7 vols. Paris: Firmin Didot, 1973 and 1975.

Malendoma, Timothée. "Les Problèmes generaux de l'économie Centrafricaine," *Europe-France-Outre-Mer* (Paris) 444 (January 1967):23–25.

O'Toole, Thomas. "Bangui, Central African Republic: A Study in Primacy, Economic and Social Development." In *Contemporary Issues in African Urbanization and Planning,* edited by R. A. Obudho, et al. Albany, New York: State University of New York Press, 1986.

______. "Shantytowns in Bangui, Central African Republic: A Cause for Despair or a Creative Possibility?" In *Slum and Squatter Settlement in Sub-Saharan Africa: Towards a Planning Strategy,* edited by R. A. Obudho and Constance C. Mhlanga. New York: Praeger, 1986.

Patassé, Ange. "La Production agricole et ses perspectives." *Europe-France-Outre-Mer* (Paris) 444 (January 1967):26–29.

Prioul, Christian. "Les Cultures maraîchères à Bangui." *Cahiers d'Outre-Mer* 86 (1969):191–202.

______. "L'Industrie et le commerce en République Centrafricaine. *Cahiers d'Outre-Mer* 88 (October-December 1969):408–429.

Yangongo, Barthélemy. "La Succession d'états en matière de biens et lettres publiques en Afrique Equatoriale." Doctoral thesis, Jean-Bedel Bokassa University, 1976.

Quarterly Economic Review of Gabon, Congo, Cameroon, Central African Republic, Chad, Equatorial Guinea. London: The Economist Intelligence Unit, published quarterly and annually.

PEOPLE AND CULTURE

Adrien-Rongier, Marie-France. "Les Kodro de Bangui: Un espace urbain 'oublié'." *Cahiers d'études Africaines* 21 (1981):43–110.

Depret, René. *Bangui: urbanisme et habitat.* Paris: Secretariat des Missions d'Urbanisme et Habitat, 1967.

Evans-Pritchard, E. E. *Witchcraft, Oracles and Magic Among the Azande.* Oxford: University Press, 1976.

Gide, André. *Voyage au Congo.* Paris: Gallimard, 1927.

Gosselin, Gabriel. *Travail et changement social en pays Gbaya (RCA).* Paris: Librairie D. Klincksieck, 1972.

Hewlett, Barry et al. "Exploration Ranges of Aka Pygmies of the Central African Republic." *Man,* n.s. 17 (1983):418–430.

Ilanga-Kabongo. "Ethnicity, Social Classes and the State in the Congo," unpublished Ph.D. dissertation, Department of Political Science, University of California, Berkeley, 1973.

Maran, René. *Batouala.* Paris: Albin Michel, 1921.

Prioul, Christian. "Le Role des relations familiales entre Bangui et les villages Centrafricaines." *Canadian Journal of African Studies* 5 (1971):61–78.

Renouf-Stefanik, Suzanne. *Animisme et Islam chez les Manza (Centrafrique). Influence de la religion Musulmane sur les coutumes traditionnelles Manya.* Paris: Société d'Etudes Linguistiques et Anthropologiques de France, 1978.

Retel-Laurentin, André. *Un Pays à la dérive: Une société en régression démographique. Les Nzakara de l'est Centrafricain.* Paris: Jean-Pierre Delarge, 1979.

Sevy, Gabriel V. *Terre Ngbaka: Etudes de l'évolution de la culture materielle d'une population forestière de RCA.* Paris: Société d'Etudes Linguistiques et Anthropologiques de France, 1972.

Thomas, Jacqueline. *Les Ngbaka de la Lobaye: Le Dépeuplement rural chez une population forestière de la République Centrafricaine.* Paris: Editions Mouton, 1963.

Vidal, Pierre. *Garçons et Filles: Le Passage à l'age d'homme chez les Gbaya Kara.* Paris: Payot, 1976.

Abbreviations and Acronyms

ACCT	Agence de Coopération Culturelle et Technique
AEF	Afrique Equatoriale Française
ANECA	Association Nationale des Etudiants Centrafricains
BCEAC	Banque Centrale des Etats de l'Afrique Centrale
BCEAO	Banque Centrale des Etats de l'Afrique Ouest
BEAC	Banque des Etats de l'Afrique Centrale
CAR	Central African Republic
CEEAC	Communauté Economique des Etats de l'Afrique Centrale
CFA	Colonies Françaises d'Afrique, then Communauté Financière Africaine
CIC	Comptoir Israëlo-Centrafricain
CMRN	Comité Militaire de Redressement National
CNTC	Confédération Nationale des Travailleurs Centrafricains
CPP	Conseil Politique Provisoire
DDI	Diamond Distributors Incorporated
ECCA/ECOCAS	Economic Community of Central African States
EEC	European Economic Community

FAC	Fonds d'Aide et Coopération
FAO	Food and Agricultural Organization
FIDES	Fonds d'Investissement pour le Développement Economique et Social
FLO	Front de Libération des Oubanguiens
FPO-PT	Front Patriotique Oubanguien-Parti du Travail
GDP	gross domestic product
GIR	Groupement Indépendant de Reflexion
GNP	gross national product
ILO	Intergroupe Libéral Oubanguien
IMF	International Monetary Fund
JPN	Jeunesse Pionnière Nationale
MCLN	Mouvement Centrafricain de Libération Nationale
MDI	Mouvement pour la Démocratie et l'Indépendance
MEDAC	Mouvement d'Evolution Démocratique de l'Afrique Centrale
MESAN	Mouvement d'Evolution Sociale de l'Afrique Noire
MLPC	Mouvement de Libération du Peuple Centrafricain
MRP	Mouvement Républicain Populaire
OAU	Organization of African Unity
OCAM	Organisation Commune Africaine et Malgache (1965–1970); Organisation Commune Africaine et Mauricienne (after 1970)
PRC	Parti Révolutionaire Centrafricain
RDA	Rassemblement Démocratique Africain
Socoulolé	Société Coopérative de l'Oubangui-Lobaye-Lessé
UAM	Union Africaine et Malgache
UCC	Union Cotonnière Centrafricaine
UDC	Union Démocratique Centrafricaine
UDEAC	Union Douanière et Economique de l'Afrique Centrale

UDSR	Union Démocratique et Sociale de la Résistance
UEAC	Union des Etats de l'Afrique Centrale
UGTCA	Union Générale des Travailleurs Centrafricains
UNDP	United Nations Development Program
UTA	Union de Transport Aérien

Index